Applied psychology and allied professions working with ethnic minorities

Edited by

Dr Yetunde Ade-Serrano
and Dr Ohemaa Nkansa-Dwamena

BPS Division of Counselling Psychology

© The British Psychological Society 2020

The views presented in this book do not necessarily reflect those of the British Psychological Society, and the publishers are not responsible for any error of omission or fact. The British Psychological Society is a registered charity (no. 229642).

British Library Cataloguing-in-Publication Data

A catalogue record for this book is available from the British Library.

ISBN 978-1-85433-780-1

Published by
The British Psychological Society
St Andrews House
48 Princess Road East
Leicester LE1 7DR
www.bps.org.uk

Contents

About the Contributors

Dr Yetunde Ade-Serrano is a chartered and registered Counselling Psychologist who works primarily in Independent Practice. She is a mentor, visiting lecturer, clinical supervisor and an external examiner on DPsych training programmes. Her clinical interests include self-exploration and growth, black women's identity, African Psychology and Spirituality, and working with race and difference across cultures.

Dr Roxane L. Gervais is a Chartered Psychologist who provides consultancy services to organisations. She uses an evidenced-based approach to address their work-related concerns; inclusive of occupational safety and health issues, to promote safe and healthy work practices. She is an invited speaker at conferences and has led projects internationally.

Dr Lorraine Gordon is a Consultant Counselling Psychologist, and former Head of Service for over five years for an Integrated Psychological Therapies Team based at the Maudsley Hospital in London. Lorraine works with adults with complex and severe mental health needs including mood, anxiety, trauma and personality difficulties. She has previously enjoyed working with psychosis having led psychology in an early intervention in psychosis service whilst working in East London. She also teaches.

Dr Masrita Ishaq is a BPS chartered Counselling Psychologist and HCPC registered practitioner psychologist. She came to the UK from Malaysia, South East Asia at the age of 15 and developed a keen interest in culture and race. She is interested in trauma, specifically transgenerational and interpersonal violence. Her background in clinical practice thus far has been in the area of complex mental health.

Faisal Mahmood is a UKCP registered individual and group gestalt psychotherapist and BACP Registered Accredited Counsellor. He is also a UKCP approved clinical supervisor. He works as a senior lecturer in counselling/psychotherapy at Newman University (Birmingham) heading up two postgraduate programmes; MSc Integrative Counselling & Psychotherapy and Advanced Diploma in Integrative Psychotherapy (UKCP accredited). He has over 20 years of experience.

Dr Erica Mapule McInnis is a Chartered Clinical Psychologist (UK), and Director and Principal Clinical Psychologist for Nubia Wellness and Healing. She specialised in online African Psychology emotional wellness courses, is a Churchill Fellow, and is the developer of 'Know Thy Self – Adinkra Cards' (an African centred therapy engagement tool with other applications). She has 22 years NHS experience and is an occasional lecturer on university clinical psychology training programmes.

Professor Zenobia Nadirshaw is a Consultant Clinical Psychologist, academician, external examiner and author of several publications on double discrimination relating to mental health and intellectual disabilities, winner of several awards including City of London award and the MBE.

Dr Ohemaa Nkansa-Dwamena is a BPS chartered Counselling Psychologist and an HCPC registered practitioner psychologist. She is a lecturer on the counselling psychology programme at City, University of London. She works primarily in independent practice with former clinical positions in NHS, higher education and third sector settings. Her research interests include multiple identity negotiation in Black individuals and culture and diversity in the therapeutic process.

Yannick Nyah is the founding board member and director at BME Volunteers Community Interest Company as well as at BlackMajor. Multiple experiences have led to his career choice. This is included in this bio to campaign for acceptance, inclusion and transparency for anyone living and navigating through various challenges.

Dr Dwight Turner is Senior Lecturer within the School of Applied Social Sciences at the University of Brighton and is also a psychotherapist and supervisor in private practice, and a part-time lecturer at the CCPE, in London. He is contactable via his website www.dwightturnercounselling.co.uk

Foreword

Yetunde Ade-Serrano & Ohemaa Nkansa-Dwamena

This publication is part of a series commissioned by the Division of Counselling Psychology. The construction of 'Working with ethnic minorities' commenced at the end of 2017. As with any publication, it has been a journey to ensuring authenticity is captured within the various narratives and best practice is highlighted for both the learning and professional growth of readers.

It is now 2020. We have completed our editorial review and submitted to the Society for publication. The environment is plastered with global unrest: Covid-19 has taken hold of the world and the murder of George Floyd although not an unfamiliar occurrence in the Black community, has become a catalyst for racial discrimination awakening. Some might state that this publication is timely; we would argue that its relevance is timeless. A racial discrimination awakening is a novel experience for some. For BME individuals, it is a different iteration of a process that has become all too familiar.

There is no homogeneity to 'our' experiences as minority ethnic people but yet we and others assemblage us together under the one banner (BME/BAME). Historically the inclusion of cultures and ethnicities under the one umbrella facilitated a unified voice in tackling racial discrimination quite rightly however it failed to nurture the validity and variety of ingroup differences. Furthermore, we miss the subtle levels of discrimination that can also occur within minority ethnic groups. The papers within this book serve to highlight idiosyncratic identities, illuminate unique stories and explore varied approaches in working relationally with individuals from differing ethnic backgrounds.

Systemic racial discrimination is much deeper than this foreword can cater for. A number of recent reports (racial disparity report, David Lammy report, Windrush report, Macgregor Smith report and the Public Health England Covid-19 report) in the UK have repeatedly highlighted the lack of equity primarily for people of Black descent particularly of African origin. Yet, we are propelled to at least dismantle some of the narratives being circulated in the current times – narratives that attempt to pinpoint poverty, social and economic differences, variations in educational attainment, nutritional deprivation, biological susceptibility to disease, etc. These narratives only serve to hide the true causes of the disease called racism. It fails to humanise Black people in the way that it limits the narrative to some of these explanations. It also perpetuates a trope that all ethnic minorities experience racism and discrimination in the same form – the danger of a single story as coined by the Nigerian writer Chimamanda Adichie.

Working with Ethnic Minorities thus serves as a point of reference in working ethically, giving consideration to the multiple levels of 'unrobing' that needs to occur as a consequence of locality, appreciating the nuances of identity and intersectionality, and building these in within clinical work, giving space for individuals to tell their own stories and endeavouring to provide a psychological service that embraces these stories in a way that is helpful to the growth of the individual and them living in the world.

We thank all contributors for your work given without hesitation, to the Society for publishing and to the Division of Counselling Psychology for commissioning these series of work.

Introduction

Dwight Turner

I need to begin this introduction with a story. When I first read this important set of chapters, one word in particular stood out for me; the word was Enculturation. Something about this word bothered me, as if I needed to investigate its meaning, and ascertain its relevance to my reading of these chapters in this volume. On discovering the meaning, I was a little taken aback realising that enculturation is the process by which an individual, or collective, learns the traditional content of a culture and assimilates its practices and values (Oxford Languages, 2012).

Enculturation though is not as common a process as one might assume. Here in the Global North we have witnessed the fear of enculturation, a fear of the approach of another culture or race, a fear which fueled the inevitable march towards the political nationalism of Brexit and the rise of White Supremacy in the USA (Bobo, 2017; Boffey, 2018). Enculturation in the meeting of the racial other is therefore the anthesis of nationalism. Nationalism abhors the change of its racialised status when it encounters difference. It resists it, pushes against it, or rises above it to seduce, to educate, to ultimately rule.

Yet, the racial other is here, so how do we survive within such a political and cultural landscape. Maya Angelou (Angelou, 1984) used to tell the story where to be black at home meant that one could be oneself. The ways we related to each other, spoke with each other, joked with each other, all held resonances of the black, or non-white, environments we felt most comfortable in. Yet, as soon as we left home, we changed. We adapted ourselves to the world of whiteness. We bowed our heads lest we were seen as a threat, we changed our language so we could be understood and seen as intelligent (or maybe even subservient), we denied our racial otherness in order, so as to not offend those whose world we had entered.

These kinds of adaptations also exist for psychology trainees and practitioners of a different racial background, and enculturation is not the route they are encouraged to follow in order to pass and become a practitioner. Instead they taught to correct their behaviour in order to fit in and feel accepted. Much like in my own field of psychotherapy, there is the unconscious encouragement to shed the racial cloak of self-identity and adopt the bleached adaptation of the profession we have all chosen to inhabit. Yet, this change, this contortion from the roots of truth which ground one's own racial identity, into the masquerade of stereotypical whiteness is not without problems, both psychological as well as physical.

That there is a fear, a pain, and even the sadness, of entering predominantly white spaces within the world of psychology is an undeniable and often researched topic within psychology. The adaptations are driven because of the systemic nature of the avoidance, ignorance and oppression raised against us. They are driven not so much by the unconscious biases of the majority culture, but the underlying fear and shame of the prejudices and hatred said culture holds (as do we all). For example, at a recent clinical psychology event a group of trainers had to apologise for their thoughtlessness in holding a mock slave auction as part of the entertainment, leading black trainees to ask if clinical psychology is a safe space to be black (Busby, 2019). That this 'performance' was authorised at all, says less about the said organiser's unconscious biases towards the racial others attending the event, but more about their unprocessed fear of and rage towards racial difference.

For the racial other there is a sense of being if not denigrated, like the experiences of those witnessing said presentation, then unseen, or silenced. There is an attempt to feel safe in white environments, yet the cost of such actions is deeply physical, sometimes psychological, and often both. These costs should not be underestimated. In a similar fashion to how internalised oppression leads to neurological problems for women, the enduring experiences of systemic racism also cause complications to men and women of colour, be they increased levels of obesity, higher blood pressure, etc. (Butler et al., 2002; Fredrickson & Harrison, 2005; Tull et al., 1999). Yet, there is a way out.

Although in no way a perfect theory, what Standpoint Theory also has to offer the world of psychology is the ingredients which could, in that it recognises the relevance and importance of the alternative, previously silenced, voices (Harding, 2004). These voices have much to offer psychology though. For example, they would allow us to decolonise how we teach psychology, how we practice our work, and how we engage with the racial other are essential aspects of this move abroad from the shores of whiteness (Nakata et al., 2012). It is this shift in perspective which makes these chapters contained in this volume so interesting, which makes them so very, very important. From encouraging the importance of a more Afro-centric perspective to the world of psychology, to considering how the experiences of BME clients with Learning Difficulties may differ to those from other racial backgrounds, to recognising the psychological importance of mentoring and mirroring for BME trainees and practitioners, what these chapters have to offer is a different voice, a different no less dominant position upon ideas and ways of being which meet the needs of their particular communities. It is important to notice though, that these chapters would not have been possible were each of these wonderful writers, and the editors of this volume, fully adapted into the dominant racial discourse within psychology. And psychology would have sacrificed itself against the alter of sameness, yet again.

To be true to the word therefore, enculturation should consequently be less about the adoption of the ethos, values and tropes forming the pillars of the dominant racial culture. No, they should really involve the growth from without one's own racial ground, where the incorporation of the external racial cultural framework of the other enhances and builds upon the structures and being of the culture of psychology. To be truly inclusive, both cultures therefore need to be open to change. The white environs of psychology need to be more open and willing to endure the pain of processing their own privilege and otherness as much as those from a different racial background. As Hegel (1976) recognised, there needs to be a recognition that culture, and this includes organisational culture, is not a fixed point. That it is a constantly changing river, careening back and forth as flows downhill towards the unifying ocean beyond. It is therefore my pleasure to write this introduction to this volume of very interesting, and worthwhile, chapters. These are chapters that deserve to be read and debated. These are chapters which will assist in returning to those of us who are the racial other the identity stripped away from us by the whiteness of the trainings we inhabit.

Dr Dwight Turner
Integrative Counsellor and Psychotherapist
University of Brighton
Centre for Counselling and Psychotherapy Education (CCPE)

References

Angelou, M. (1984). *I know why the caged bird sings.* USA: Virago.

Bobo, L. (2017). Racism in Trump's America: reflections on culture, sociology, ad the 2016 US presidential election. *British Journal of Sociology, 68*(S1), S85–S104. https://doi.org/10.1111/1468-4446.12324

Boffey, D. (2018, November). Empire 2.0: the fantasy that's fuelling Tory divisions on Brexit. *Guardian* Online, p.1. Retrieved from https://www.theguardian.com/politics/2018/nov/08/empire-fantasy-fuelling-tory-divisions-on-brexit

Busby, E. (2019, November). 'Shameful' Slave auction re-enactment held at UK university conference dinner. *Independent* Online, p.1. Retrieved from https://www.independent.co.uk/news/education/education-news/liverpool-university-slave-auction-conference-dinner-racism-psychology-a9203316.html

Butler, C., Tull, E.S., Chambers, E.C., Taylor, J. & Ph, D. (2002). Internalised racism, body fat distribution, and abnormal fasting glucose among caribbean women in Dominica, West Indies. *Journal of the National Medical Association, 94*(3), 143–148.

Fredrickson, B.L. & Harrison, K. (2005). Throwing like a girl: Self-objectification predicts adolescent girls' motor performance. *Journal of Sport & Social Issues, 29*(1), 79–101. https://doi.org/10.1177/0193723504269878

Harding, S. (2004). *The Feminist standpoint theory reader.* New York and London: Routledge.

Hegel, G. (1976). *Phenomenology of spirit.* USA: Oxford University Press.

Nakata, N.M., Nakata, V., Keech, S. & Bolt, R. (2012). Decolonial goals and pedagogies for Indigenous studies. *Decolonization: Indigeneity, Education & Society, 1*(1), 120140.

Oxford Languages. (2012). Oxford English Dictonary. UK: Oxford University Press.

Tull, S.E., Wickramasuriya, T., Taylor, J. et al. (1999). Relationship of internalized racism to abdominal obesity and blood pressure in Afro-Caribbean women. *Journal of the National Medical Association, 91*(8), 447–452. Retrieved from http://www.pubmedcentral.nih.gov/articlerender.fcgi?artid=2608441&tool=pmcentrez&rendertype=abstract

'I'm not your minority – Know Thy African Self'

Erica Mapule McInnis

Universal practice of Eurocentric psychology does not promote wellness and resilience effectively enough in those of African heritage. Incorporation of the best of African culture is proposed as a wellness strategy to counter 'reliance on the psychology that enslaved us to save us.' Healing strategies which pre-dated colonisation and maintained ancestors through significant trauma offer a valuable addition to the therapist's toolkit. This chapter is written with the African therapist in mind as there is too little devotion to their needs, given both the anticipated and desired increase in therapists of African origin. Furthermore, the need for those of African heritage to progress to the stage where they offer something other than what white therapists offer, with a black face.

The aim of this chapter is to introduce the paradigm of African psychology and accompanying therapy, with discussion in a black British context. Emotional Emancipation Circles (EEM SM) are suggested as a first line of defence alongside strategies for inclusion of African Centred approaches in the therapy room as a second line of defence. The chapter concludes with exploration of concepts from an African worldview, posing the question 'who really is the minority'. To continue to drink from the deep well of African thought is proposed as a transformational practice and 'a call to action (Akoben)' for healing for Afrikans who wish to hear the call.

Questions:

1. How do you connect in therapy with clients whose ancestors originate in Africa?
2. If you do, how do you know how African they are in their orientation?
3. Why is it important to focus on the needs of black[1] clients?

This chapter will introduce with urgency:
- the paradigm of African psychology (also known as Afrikan/African centred psychology, Africana psychology, Afrocentric psychology)
- application of such approaches to illuminate and transform clients at both a community and individual level
- use of this approach in the therapy room.

---

[1]   Use of the term Black, African and Afrikan is interchangeable in this chapter as inspired by the author. However, it is acknowledged it is still a point of contention for some. Some see them as completely interchangeable, others distinct as to call ourselves African crucially emphasises the relationship with the continent of Africa and its practices rather than a grouping based on colour of skin (Cokley & Garba, 2018).

This is so that the paradigm of African psychology is available to the competent therapist's toolkit as a resource to understand and elevate the experiences of Afrikans[2]. This chapter makes no apology for its focus upon facilitating black (Afrikan) therapists working with black clients, for unless they have an alternative to a European/ western paradigm to operate from, they will only replicate limitations of Eurocentric approaches with a black face. The point of diversifying the workforce thus lost. Of course, concepts can be applied to others oppressed or not eu-melaninated in a similar fashion to how Eurocentric/western concepts are applied to black people.

Why is it important to focus on the needs of black clients?
Relating to blackness

Relating to blackness in therapy comes with imagined and sometimes real risks when clinicians are socialised and often reinforced through training to view western assessment techniques and therapies as the gold standard for healing all people. Many therapists fear instant dismissal or failure of a placement for just being 'too black with their black clients', talking street talk, Black Vernacular Language, proverbs or patios. This is when these very acts may benefit and assist black people to feel heard, share a common language of expression, and tap into culture wisdom in the therapy room.

Despite challenges and obstacles to negotiate, there is an outstanding need for our people to be introduced to therapies which stem from an alternative to a western world view in order to save and enhance their souls. From the disproportionate number of black people in psychological distress, western approaches either are not doing this quickly enough or not at all. Many Afrikans suffer combat fatigue from frequent micro-aggressions, macro-aggressions, vicarious trauma and more (Thomas, 2016). Some therapists may find or create opportunities to apply African centred therapy in statutory services such as the NHS (National Health Service). Others take freedom in private (independent) practice to relate to their clients from a perspective which makes sense to both. The NHS (National Health Service) and other statutory western orientated providers will eventually catch up, but will we as black people still be here by then?

What do we add? Empowered and supported African centred therapists allow clients the opportunity to explore how the system of white supremacy influences their lived situation. Black therapists can exhibit genuine empathy from being in the shoes of the client and discuss problem solving from an informed position.

African centred therapy in a Black British context

In McInnis (2018), the heterogeneity of black people living in Britain is explored. Lennox (2013) explains foundations for relational problems from generations of family separations in race based chattel enslavement. This pattern replicated by the Windrush generation who between the 1940s and 1970s left the West Indies and Caribbean islands to travel to serve the country they were taught was their 'mother country' leaving behind young children some sent for, some not. Elements repeated when families from the West Indies, Caribbean and Africa separate in contemporary times seeking economic survival and opportunities.

---

[2] Afrikan (Wilson 1993) those with eu-melanin (high skin pigmentation which causes Afrikan features) and of African heritage.

Thwarted ambitions, degradations, overt and covert abuses and threats of deporta-
tion of family members due to government policy changes (Serwotka 2018) contribute
to emotions ripe for processing in the therapy room. Otherwise there is the likelihood
such emotions become patterns of disproportionate: dysfunctional family functioning,
prison and inpatient mental health detention, self-medication with drugs and alcohol,
and lower sustained senior management or leadership roles (Thomas, 2016). Using
African psychology provides a framework to explore such issues and goes beyond 'how
we are' to a spiritual way we can affirm, repair, reclaim and resist.

Therapists wanting to relate to black people cannot rely on the therapy room.
By then it may be too late. Many to be healed can't afford to attend individual
therapy and those who can, may choose not. They may fear or experience psychological analysis which does little to understand their lived experiences (let alone
distress) and some may feel re-traumatised when they come into contact with
mental health services. Unfortunately, the black community is often socialised
to be materialistic, with members funding a music concert or the latest fashion
of trainers (sneakers) rather than psychological therapy. This is indicative of the
'commodification of self' versus the 'care of self'.

How do you relate in therapy with clients whose ancestors originate in Africa?
What is African Psychology?

African Psychology[3] situates the examination of human behaviour within an
African worldview drawing on the best of African philosophy, African traditional
religion, African traditional medicine and healing systems, self-knowledge and
intuition. It uses (but is not limited) to these for interpreting, understanding
and elevating the African in the diaspora and on the continent of Africa (Grills,
2018; Karenga, 2010). It acknowledges that not all African practices were good
(as with all cultures) but proposes addition of their best to a toolkit. It acknowledges variation needed to apply in a modern day context, as what benefitted then
may not enhance now. A comprehensive definition of Black/African psychology is
presented by Parham, White and Ajamu (1999, p.95) and is accepted as the official
definition by the Association of Black Psychologists (ABPsi).[4]

Common to all definitions is the emphasis on:
- the living conditions in which Black people (Afrikans) exist (cultural context)
- the heightened experiences of worldwide oppression of Black people
  (Afrikans) and understandings of self-introduced from such experiences
- the need to advance Black communities, not just individuals, given the disproportionate numbers of individuals of African descent in adverse settings
- remembering and implementing the best practices from the continent of
  Africa prior to colonisation and race specific chattel enslavement as tools for
  wellness. For example, Ma'at (Karenga 2004) from ancient Egypt and Adinkra
  symbols from west African.

---

[3] A summary of the origins of African Psychology can be found in Jamison (2018) and Karenga
(2010) amongst others.
[4] This is a USA based international organisation with a purpose and mission to advance African
psychology, assist solving problems within black communities from a perspective highly relevant
to them, liberate the African mind, empower the African character, enliven and illuminate the
African spirit.

- the impact of eumelanin (the chemical that causes brown and black skin pigmentation) on the mind, body, spirit and behaviour of individuals
- the development of multi-dimensional understandings of self beyond a westernised perspective as a tool for resistance and transformation (progression)
- illuminating the spiritual self, ancestral connecting for protecting and finding one's spiritual purpose
- the introduction of unresolved, but resolvable, intergenerational trauma within black communities from: the Maafa (Afrikan holocausts such as from the transatlantic chattel slave trade and colonisation) and human made disasters predominantly affecting former colonised nations. These co-exist with insurmountable resilience
- di-unital thinking in terms of events being both good and bad at the same time (i.e. a union of opposites)
- benefits of self-definition rather than pure restriction to other's concepts for description, revision and transformation to our best personhood (becoming better)
- the relationship between individuals and connecting with others as a primary African centred value (Myers, 1993).

According to Karenga (2010) the three major schools of black/African psychology are Traditional, Reformist and Radical (with a good recent summary found in Cokley and Garba 2018). Essentially, the Traditional school supports the Eurocentric model with minor changes such as for racial bias, for example Cognitive Behaviour Therapy for Black people. The Reformist school focuses upon changes in public policy. The Radical school adopts an African centred framework, not attempting to appeal to white people but rather focus on transforming the attitude of black people towards themselves. As I grew as a psychologist, I became a pupil of the Radical school, thus this chapter is heavily influenced by such a perspective.

African Centred Therapy (African Therapy)
Core concepts underpinning African Centred Therapy include:
1. facilitating ability to 'know thy self' (multi-dimensional self-knowledge)
2. illuminating the self-healing human spirit
3. enhancing the spirit of Ubuntu (individuals relating to each other collectively in a community using values such as caring, compassion and hospitality) and
4. manifesting the role of ancestors in the here and now (Nobles et al., 2016; Parham, 2002a). This is within a framework of African centred cultural principles, understandings, norms and/or traditions. There are specific African centred therapies derived from African psychology such as Belief Systems Analysis (BSA) (Myers, 1999) which specifically stems from her Optimal Psychology Theory (Myers, 1993). In this approach the therapist builds a relationship with the client so the client can explore and contrast their worldview (belief system) with an African centred belief system. This is to (as benefits the client), move away from limitations from a western/Eurocentric worldview towards benefits from an ancient African

worldview.[5] Thus, understanding a client's worldview and how oppression and suboptimal thinking contributes to their psychological distress leads to developing a spiritual base, further self-knowledge, illumination and transformation of the self to assist negotiating the challenges of life (Myers et al., 2018).

In addition to structured African centred approaches such as BSA (Myers, 1993), there are less prescriptive ways of being African centred in therapy which may suit the needs of some clients and therapists. This often involves exploring and encouraging:

1. African cultural principles and understandings,
2. African concepts of self, person and health and
3. Relating to energy and nature as spiritually (intuitively) guided depending upon what comes to the therapist in the moment in the therapy room (Grills and Ajei, 2002, Obasi, 2002).

This can stem from material brought into therapy and the therapist's reflections between therapeutic encounters. Personal therapy and supervision is encouraged to safeguard against the therapist's own unresolved issues unhelpfully influencing practice.

Why is this form of relating needed? For many black people western psychological therapies are incongruent with their Afrikan cultures, lived experiences, inter-generational traumas and loss of protective ancient cultural knowledge. Affirming cultural knowledge and passing on cultural wisdom for navigating life is essential for the survival of any nation and often lost through the process of enslavement and colonisation. Indeed, displaced people often lack their true surnames which with each signature written can serve as reminders of prior location, roles and destiny (Nubia, 2017).

A coping strategy of acculturation (which can be trying to be White to avoid oppression), lays a firm foundation for dis-at-ease (psychological distress). In Patois (a language widely spoken in Jamaica and other Caribbean countries) the author summarises this as:

'after yu bruk up yu self and twist up yu-self to mek yu-self fit inna what was never meant fi yu, yu is truly bruk-up'

'This is even before dem spit you out as yu a occupy space reserved for the white people dem'.

(Translated as 'after you break yourself and mould yourself to fit into a situation not designed for you to advance, you become really ill. This is even before you get chucked out as you occupy a position reserved for a white person.')

---

[5] A western/Eurocentric approach tends to focus on materialism, segmented parts, counting and measuring, highest value in acquisition of objects and competition is considered for black people sub-optimal functioning (Myers, 1988). African centred worldview (Kambon, 1998) has a traditional focus on: spiritual, holistic, self knowledge, highest value in positive interpersonal relationships, communalism and oneness with nature (considered for black people optimal functioning, Myers, 1988).

How do you know how African orientated your client is?
Spotting the client ripe for African centred thinking in therapy?

Declaring an African centred approach may frighten some clients and indeed would have frightened me before my development from a psychologist who happens to be black, to one who is 'woke' (also known as conscious). 'Woke' being defined as African centred/Pan African in all aspects of life, as the progress of both my community and self-determines. The question arises, how do you know how African centred you can be with the black client who walks into the therapy room? There can be obvious indicators (for those enlightened), such as recognising:

- African centred jewellery such as the Ankh or Gye Name symbol
- African cultural clothing such as wearing of kente or mud cloth
- natural hair styles such as locks
- name changes to symbolic African names
- cultural festivals observed such as Kwanzaa.

However, this all depends on the therapist having reached a level of 'wokeness' to recognise the code within such symbols. Then if the therapist has picked up on the conscious code, are they able, supported and confident enough to relate to them? Furthermore, how truly Afrikan is the client who has the above? Are they just sporting a headstyle (hairstyle) in fashion or drinking so deep from the well of Afrikan consciousness that they reject Eurocentric images of beauty not only at an outer but inner level?

Finding this out can be a process of 'try it and see', but there are African centred models and measures to assist this journey (Kambon, 1999; Kambon & Bowen-Reid, 2010). For those lacking appreciation of their African identity, informing them you wish to apply models based on the best of African culture may stimulate horror, fear and even a request to be given western models and treated the same as White people (even if to their own detriment). For some a journey can sensitively be made perhaps in response to indications they are open to reflect upon how their race, multiple cultures and family experiences (which often span continents) interact with their wellbeing. This is helped by building a relationship where identifying difference is not seen as done to initiate inferior interventions, but rather culturally enhanced and syntonic work (Jackson-Lowman, 2014). Conversations about common experiences between the therapist and client while 'living while black' can aid clients bringing these experiences into the therapy room. It is of note, some black people can be African orientated in some aspects of their being but not others. Furthermore, in a UK context there may be identification with for example the Caribbean, which does not yet extend as far back as Africa.

In addition to models for understanding, there are measures to be administered directly to clients which indicate African orientation such as the Belief Systems Analysis Scale (BSAS) (Montgomery et al., 1990). This can be used as a short cut to gauge how African centred the person may be initially and at different stages in therapy. In addition, experienced African centred therapists are likely to form an opinion on how African centred to be with a client intuitively, as inspired from teachings such as New Visions for Black Men (Akbar, 2016) which is equally applicable to black women.

Nosology (classification of diseases) from an African centred perspective is beyond the scope of this chapter but also offers worthy alternatives for understanding 1. how black people come to be in the state they are in, 2. why they remain there, and 3. strategies to generate meaningful interventions for them which add understanding to lives and can help shift feelings (Akbar, 1998; Kambon, 1999; Azibo, 2014). This is to transform feelings of confusion, bewilderment and sometimes disappointment at not achieving when one is blessed to be in the 'so called first world' (which from an African centred perspective could not be 'first' as the ancient African world pre-dates, Ani ,1994). Cultural understanding of your client brings relating.

Relating through Emotional Emancipation Circles (EEMSM) and Individual Therapy

The black therapist relating to the black community needs to be armed with therapy as both a preventive and reactive weapon of choice. Therefore, the first line of defence for the black population becomes interventions such as Emotional Emancipation Circles (EECSM) (Grills et al., 2016) (free community healing circles) which follow a template developed by the Association of Black Psychologists (ABPsi) and Community Healing Network (CHN). This is where black people come together in safe spaces to unlock keys and:

- Share their stories
- Deepen their understanding of the legacy of enslavement and colonisation upon their emotional lives
- Learn essential emotional wellness skills and
- Tell themselves new liberating and empowering stories about who they are as people of African ancestry

Black therapists are in an ideal position to train to facilitate and evaluate such groups. This is because promoting wellness in the wider community arms it with resilience skills for future traumas and goes some way to healing past traumas. Many black therapists were amongst community members who attended an EECSM I ran in Brixton, London (UK) in 2018/2019 and often shared stories of facing pressures in high status demanding roles with a search for ongoing culturally relevant support. In feedback gained halfway through, 73 per cent reported finding it an 'Excellent' resource on their journey to improved wellness. Furthermore, 94 per cent reported it either 'Excellent or Good' in adding to their existing skills and knowledge.

The second line of defence[6] becomes individual therapy. Many black middle class professionals experience trauma when they realise utopia or Wakanda[7] does not come from gaining qualifications, affluence, fancy job titles and moving further from the 'hood'/'ghetto'/'black areas'. In my independent clinical practice, I receive many requests from black professionals who function with depression and anxiety as they 'hang on' in their increasingly white spaces. This is in addition

---

[6] Neeley Fuller Jr (1972/ 2016) gives the analogy black people are surviving behind enemy lines, born into a war zone of a system of white (or the whitest) supremacy where some experience greater levels of confinement but all are confined.

[7] Wakanda is a depiction of a fictional Africa never colonised by Europeans complete with enhancing African cultural practices. It is admired for its great technological advances and wealth superior to the West and popularised in the film 'Black Panther' released in the UK. (2018).

to members of the black community who in addition to blackness; experience oppression from poverty, class, disability, sexuality and more.

It is of note, even in black majority environments or those with black leadership; the standards to which they aspire or are held accountable may be Eurocentric. In my own practice I carefully include Eurocentric measures alongside African centred approaches to evaluate transformation in clients. Being African centred is about taking the best from all cultures including my own so an African centred approach can be enhanced by Eurocentric additions.

African Centred Therapy in practice

For clients at a stage in their personality development where they are essentially orientated to want to be a white person in black skin (Kambon & Reid, 2010), only the minor features of an African centred approach may be tolerated. Just to 'be' with the client in therapy may assist them to open up about tensions navigating their black space in white controlled environments. They may not be at a stage where they can make changes such as to leave toxic environments or gain wellness from cultural congruence found from bringing their full self into environments, rather than just the bits they feel 'massa[8]' will tolerate. Attachment issues which stem from transmitted ancestral experiences during enslavement and colonisation can affect the ability of many black clients to trust and relate to any therapist (Davids, 2011; Fletchman-Smith, 2011).

For clinicians wishing to become more African centred in their practice the following is offered to assist relating to clients:

- Placing affirming African imagery in the therapy room, reception and waiting areas. This includes pictures, small or large ornaments, with small pieces being portable between different therapy rooms.
- If inspired, wear jewellery or clothes with African imagery a client may comment on and thus stimulate conversation. This can communicate to the client where you are on your journey to prompt sharing. The deep structure being African clothing helps clients see the therapist as healthy and well-adjusted which serves as a re-Africanising experience (Cabral, 1974).
- To aid expression of self, be open to use with a client, cultural sayings, proverbs, black vernacular language, street talk or any shared cultural language (Goddard et al., in submission).
- Use African concepts as a tool for engagement in therapy. In my own therapeutic practice symbolic or written methods can help engagement such as: 1. Adinkra symbols – wisdom in symbol form from traditional Old Kingdoms of West Africa (www.nubiawellnessandhealing.co.uk/adinkra-cards) 2. Transformation cards which use images both from ancient Egypt and relevant to Afrikans (www.neferatitiife.co.uk) and 3. 'Mama Used to Say' cards of Jamaican traditional wisdom sayings (www.onehandcantclap.co.uk/things-mama-used-to-say). Clients can choose cards they are attracted to, explain why and this reveals inner values for exploration or for the therapist to be aware in relating. These interventions use concepts relevant to the black lived experience. In addition to use as an assessment aid, an adjunct use may be for evaluation of therapy which may reveal changes which can indicate transformation (progress).

---

[8] 'Massa' refers to the slave master within enslavement many Afrikans still try to serve either consciously or unconsciously.

- Use of formal African centred assessment tools (Jones, 1996; Parham, 2002b).
- As appropriate introduce African cultural rituals in therapy. For example, in a session I offered, and the client accepted opening and closing libations. This was because she mentioned the death of her aunt which troubled her. As part of pouring water into a bowl to remember her ancestors she was invited to reflect on the gifts that aunt brought to her. The conversation changed from mourning to rejoicing and thanking the aunt for her teachings and recognition that she must die for others to be born with her spirit in accordance with African centred thinking about the role of ancestors.
- The client and therapist reflecting on their energy before, during and after therapy. Energy can be an indicator of spirit in action and the level of disruption or wellness in the client.
- Meditation/mindfulness at the start and end of the therapy session to help calm the mind and the body. From my own clinical practice, many clients report needing to do this before they can focus upon themselves and their experiences which are distressing and traumatic. Furthermore, to do another meditation at the end of the session limits leaving the session highly aroused and dysregulated. One does not have to be a qualified mindfulness practitioner to play a mindfulness or meditation app with a client that is appropriate for the general population. Use of meditations from meditation apps in the session can be helpful and easily found and played on a smart phone; progressing to introducing African centred meditations (Anpu, 2017). Initial work may be needed to explain African roots of meditations (Anpu, 2017). For those not yet able to identify with Africa positively or believe meditation is against their religion, the following may help. For example, for Christians offering that Jesus in the wilderness for 40 days and 40 nights entered a process to be still and reflect in a similar fashion to how individuals can report clearer thinking following even brief periods of meditation. I find clients who may be sceptical initially, when given the opportunity to repeat in regular sessions, report benefits.
- Being an activist for, with or encouraging a client to be. Continuously healing the wounds of oppression does nothing to address underlying issues, furthermore; resilience with the addition of resistance is wellness. Although openly challenging oppression can have adverse consequences, opportunities can be made or found. Indeed, resistance can be a relay race where progress is made generation by generation.

For further information on therapy from an African centred perspective please consult Parham (2002a).

Conclusions
Why am I not your minority?

In the title of this chapter is 'I'm not your minority'. Why? From a 'world perspective' black people are not an ethnic minority but an ethnic majority (Kambon, 1998) given:
- the true size, population and ethnicity of Africa
- the hue of those populating Caribbean and pacific islands
- the complexion of majority of people of South America

- the complexion of the indigenous people of Australia and New Zealand
- the complexion of many people in India and China.

To what extent do we relate to our clients as being lesser if we refer to them as minorities when they are actually a world majority? Just because colonialism indoctrinated us to measure time from a point in Europe (GMT, Greenwich Mean Time), does not mean we should consider countries and their people to only exist from the moment Europeans mis-guided themselves there with their uncivilised behaviour[9]. Furthermore, in some parts of the UK the client in front of you may well be in the ethnic majority depending on where the boundary line of the vicinity is drawn.

Also, to what extent do we limit clients when we work from an 'either or' perspective rather than a 'both and' African perspective. After all, we are working with people both welcome and not welcome in this country at the same time, experts in themselves while clueless about themselves at the same time.

How to continue to drink from the deep well of African Thought?

Attending the international convention of the Association of Black Psychologists (ABPsi) www.abpsi.org gives access to the latest thinking on application of African psychology to modern day problems. Such conventions are usually yearly in the USA. There are also the spiritual journeys which can lead to Kemetamorphosis (a rebirth in self-knowledge and affirming of the greatness from which one came) which can be found from African centred study tours of ancient Egypt and other parts of Africa. Those born in or lingering in a cold climate may need this prescription more.

For those needing to keep their feet closer to home, there are workshops and presentations on African Psychology such as by the author. University therapy training courses are awakening to the power of adding African psychology to their curriculum at all levels of training. This should be considered by students/trainees seeking the best training to meet their cultural, spiritual, cognitive and emotional needs.

The essence of African psychology is relating (synonymous with attachment in Eurocentric terms). Transformation (progress gained from life experiences or therapy) is enhancing the fabric of individuals in communities to relate to both each other and themselves in healthy and progressive ways. A healthy spirit and resulting person is defined as: confident, competent and with a sense of full possibility and unlimited potentiality (Grills et al., 2018). Health is not simply the absence of disease but a life that promotes as appropriate the best of African thinking, values, customs, genetic memory, healing practices and achieving in a way that morally (Karenga, 2004) benefits self and others.

---

[9] In reference to Christopher Columbus being lost when he discovered or re-discovered Caribbean islands naming some the West Indies as he wrongly believed himself off the coast of India.

It promotes pursuit of the best of African culture in daily life rather than purely orientating oneself to mimic 'former' colonisers warts and all. It can be done by preventative, reclaiming, repairing, resilience and wellness building strategies such as Emotional Emancipation Circles (EEM[SM]). Furthermore, individual therapy which allows the client to bring their full self into the therapy space (not just their sanctioned Eurocentric self). Afrifuturism (the future of African psychotherapy) becomes a call to reconsider the appropriateness of continuing to purely allow our coloniser's western terms to describe our healing work as psychologists. The proposed term Skh Djr (Sakhu Djaer) (Grills et al., 2018; Nobles, 2015) meaning illuminator and liberator of the spirit, identifies a further way to relate.

In concluding this chapter, this goes beyond information sharing and recommendations but is a call to action (Akoben). Unless the best of African culture is preserved and progressed as a healing paradigm, it will become a relic in a museum such as the Petrie or British museum in London, along with other artefacts as a testament to how good we once were (Akbar, 2016). If we as black people charged to be preservers of our cultures do not take action, the blueprint our ancient Egyptian ancestors diligently carved into stone to preserve for us to follow, will become the new wave of therapy others sell back to black people at inflated prices (with the spiritual key to it in master classes preserved for the elite). Let us bring the paradigm of healing back to black for those socialised to think black and African is bad. Let us remind them while the ice age took place in Europe the golden age of abundance took place in Africa. Europeans set sail in ships to take what was good while simultaneously misleading us and suggesting it was bad. For those grown to reclaim their culture for wellbeing, transformation and upliftment it becomes a question of 'to be Afrikan or not to be'.

Dr Erica Mapule McInnis
Clinical Psychologist

Dedication

This chapter is dedicated to my late father Jeremiah Eric McInnis (b.1928 – d.2017). You will never know how great you were, the legacy and path you left for me and others to follow. May our ancestors greet you well. Asante sana.

I would like to thank the following members of the Association of Black Psychologist (ABPsi) for reading and commenting on early drafts:
Dr Huberta Jackson-Lowman President of the Association of Black Psychologist (ABPsi)
Dr Wade Nobles, Professor Emeritus, Department of Africana Studies at San Francisco State University and former President of ABpsi; and
Dr Mark Bolden, Professor of Counselling, Trinity Washington University.

References

Akbar, N. (1998). *Know Thy Self*. Tallahassee, FL: Mind productions.

Akbar, N. (2016). *New visions for Black men*. Tallahassee, FL: Mind productions.

Ani, M. (1994). *Yurugu: An Afrikan-centered critique of European cultural thought and behavior*. Trenton: Africa World Press.

Anpu, U.R. (2017). *Meditations for African Americans. Igniting the inner light*. Gye Nyame: USA.

Azobo, D.A. (2014). The Azibo Nosology II: Epexegesis and 25th Anniversary Update: 55 Culture-focused Mental Disorders Suffered by African Descent People. *The Journal of Pan African Studies, vol. 7, no. 5*, 32–176.

Cabral, A. (1974). *Return to the source: Selected speeches of Amilcar Cabral*. Monthly Review Press: USA.

Cokley, K. & Garba, R. (2018). Speaking truth to power: How Black/African Psychology changed the discipline of Psychology. *Journal of Black Psychology, vol 44* (8), 695–721.

Davids, M.F. (2011). *Internal Racism a psychoanalytic approach to race and difference*. Hampshire: Palgrave Macmillan.

Fletchman-Smith, B. (2011). *Transcending the legacies of slavery: A psychoanalytic view*. Sussex: Routledge.

Fuller, Jr. N. (1972/ 2016). The United Independent Compensatory Code/System/Concept: A Compensatory Counter-Racist Code. Revised/Expanded Edition. Neeley Fuller Jr: USA

Goddard, L.L., Rowe, T.D., McInnis, E.M. & DeLoach, C.D. The Role of Proverbs in African-Centered Psychology (in submission).

Grills, C. & Ajei, M. (2002). African-centered conceptualizations of self and consciousness: The Akan model. In T. Parham (Ed.) *Counselling persons of African descent. Raising the bar of practitioner competence*. California: Sage.

Grills, C., Nobles, W.W. & Hill, C. (2018). African, Nlack, Neither or Both? Models and strategies developed and implemented by the Association of Black Psychologists. *Journal of Black Psychology, vol 44* (8), 791–826.

Grills, C.N., Aird, E.G. & Rowe, D. (2016). Breathe, baby, breathe: Clearing the way for the emotional emancipation of Black people. *Cultural Studies Critical Methodologies, 16*(3), 333–343. https://doi.org/10.1177/1532708616634839

Jackson-Lowman, H. (2014). (Ed.). A culturally-syntonic model of healthy identity for Afrikan American women. In H. Jackson-Lowman *Afrikan American women: Living at the crossroads of race, gender, class, and culture* (pp.11–26). USA: Cognella Academic Publishing.

Jamison, D.F. (2018). Key concepts, theories and issues in African/Black Psychology: A view from the bridge. *Journal of Black Psychology, vol 44* (8), 722–746.

Jones, R. L. (1996). *Handbook of tests and measurements for Black populations: volume 1*. USA: Cobb & Henry.

Kambon, K.K.K. (1999). African/Black Psychology in the American context: An African centered Approach. USA: Nubian Nation Publications.

Kambon, K.K.K. & Bowen-Reid, T. (2010). Theories of African American personality: Classification, basic constructs and empirical predictions/assessment. *The Journal of Pan African Studies, Vol 3, no 8*, 83–108.

Karenga, M. (2004). *Maat, The Moral Ideal in Ancient Egypt: A study in Classical African Ethics*. London: Routledge.

Karenga, M. (2010). *Introduction to Black studies* (4th edn). University of Sankore Press: Los Angeles.

Lennox (2013). Attachment in African Caribbean families. In A. Danquah & K. Berry *Attachment theory in adult mental health. A guide to clinical practice*. Sussex: Routledge.

McInnis, E.M. (2018). Understanding African beingness and becoming. *Therapy Today*, Oct, *29*(8), 28–31.

Montgomery, D.E., Fine, M.A. & James-Myers, L. (1990). The development and validation of an instrument to assess an optimal Afrocentric world view. *Journal of Black Psychology, 17*(1), 37–54. https://doi.org/10.1177/00957984900171004

Myers, L.J. (1993). *Understanding an Afrocentric world view: Introduction to an optimal psychology*. Iowa: Kendall Hunt.

Myers, L.J. (1999). Therapeutic processes for health and wholeness in the 21st cebtury: Belief systems analysis and the paradigm shift. In R.L. Jones *Advances in African American psychology* (pp.313–358). Hampton, VA: Cobb and Henry.

Myers, L.J., Anderson, M., Lodge, T., Speight, S. & Queener, J.E. (2018). Optimal theory's contributions to understanding and surmounting global challenges to humanity. *Journal of Black Psychology, vol 44* (8), 747–771.

Nobles, W., Baloyi, L. & Sodi, T. (2016). Pan African Humanness and Sakhu Djaer as Praxis for Indigenous Knowledge Systems. *ALTERNATION Interdisciplinary Journal for the Study of the Arts and Humanities in Southern Africa Special Edition 18,* 36–59.

Nobles, W. (2015). From Black psychology to sakhu djaer: Implications for the further development of a Pan African Black Psychology. *Journal of Black Psychology, 41,* 399–414.

Nubia, O. (2017). The power of names. Centre of Pan African Thought. https://www.panafrican-thought.com/video/the-power-of-names/ (sourced on 8 February 2019).

Obasi E.M. (2002). Reconceptualizing the notion of self from the African deep structure. In T. Parham (Ed.) *Counselling persons of African descent. Raising the bar of practitioner competence.* California: Sage.

Parham, T. (2002a). *Counselling persons of African descent. Raising the bar of practitioner competence.* California: Sage.

Parham, T. (2002b). Understanding personality and how to measure it. In T. Parham (Ed.) *Counselling persons of African descent. Raising the bar of practitioner competence.* California: Sage.

Parham, T.A., White, J.L. & Ajamu, A. (1999). *The psychology of Blacks: An African centered perspective.* USA: Pearson.

Serwotka, M. (2018). How dare ministers try to blame the Windrush fiasco on home office staff. *The Guardian* 24 April 2018. https://www.theguardian.com/commentisfree/2018/apr/24/ministers-home-office-staff-windrush-scandal-mark-serwotka

Thomas, L.K. (2016). Generationally transmitted trauma in African descended communities. Paper presented at the Association of Family Therapists (17 September 2016).

Wilson, A. (1993/2014). *The falsification of African consciousness: Eurocentric history, psychiatry and the politics of White supremacy.* New York: African World Infosystems.

Mental health in South East Asians – A spotlight on Malaysians

Masrita Ishaq

Working with diversity has always interested and eluded me, I spent much of my years in training reflecting on the impact of my evidently cultural difference on my sense of self. There has always been a draw towards understanding more about the interplay between these differences, but it also always felt like a complex and muddled subject. For me, it is difficult to reflect on my own diversity without recalling too the experiences of marginalisation and discrimination both in the UK and my home country. The latter has been the murkier. In my own journey, a part of me feels that it is an important subject yet a part of me always wondered whether I am making a big deal out of my experiences and that perhaps I have been 'too sensitive' and misunderstood others' intentions.

I spent many months grappling with how to approach this topic. I do not feel like I have achieved a sophisticated understanding of my process, yet do not want to pen an academic literature review article. I cannot write about working relationally with diversity without reflecting on my own background and experience of being a South East Asian in the UK. So, this is where I will start. Then inevitably influenced by being in this profession, I will explore common perceptions of mental health, its influence on therapy or help seeking behaviours and conclude by presenting some suggestions on therapeutic engagement with this client group. I will draw mainly from my personal experience and interweave this with literature.

Background – Malaysia

My country of birth and residence up until about fifteen years old was Malaysia; a Southeast Asian country. This region is geographically south of China and Japan and east of India. It is also to the north of Australia. Sovereign states in this region comprise of Vietnam, Laos, Cambodia, Thailand, Myanmar, Indonesia, Singapore, Philippines, Brunei Darussalam and East Timor.

Malaysia is made up of three main ethnic groups – 68.8 per cent Malay or 'Bumiputera', 23.2 per cent Chinese, 7.0 per cent Indians and 1.0 per cent Others (Department of Statistics Malaysia, 2017). The official language is Malay but English is familiar and spoken by all urban and most rural people. A mixture of the two including words from Chinese and Tamil language is termed Manglish. It is sometimes known as the unofficial language of Malaysia and used colloquially. It is spoken with an accent that can distinguish the main ethnic group and language background of the speaker (Pillai, 2008). Its use has been argued to foster a sense of identity and belonging (Ibrahim, 2005) among Malaysians. Generally, Malaysia is a collectivist culture where there is a strong emphasis on interdependent relationships with parents, family, and larger social groups with little variation between each ethnicity.

Due to the multiethnic makeup, Malaysia is also multicultural and multilingual. The original culture stemmed from indigenous tribes and Malays who are an Austronesian ethnic group that predominantly inhabit Malaysia, Indonesia, Brunei, Singapore and Southern Thailand. The common marker of Malays is the religion of Islam, Malay language and traditions although there might be slight variations between countries. During the peak of Maritime Southeast Asia around the 1400s and 1600s, Malacca (a state in Malaysia) was a centre for trade and commerce (Reid & Sportswood, 1988–1993). An imperial officer, Zheng He from China, played an integral role in expanding Malacca's influence. His involvement was also the beginning of the integration of Chinese businesspeople in Malacca. The common markers of the Chinese are spiritual and philosophical traditions of Confucianism, Daoism and Buddhism, Cantonese and Mandarin languages and traditions. Some also follow Christianity. Last but not least, the third largest ethnic group of Malaysia are the Indians and the majority follow the religion of Hindu, speak Tamil language and its associated traditions. It is not uncommon to see places of worship and national celebrations for the Malays, Chinese and Indians scattered around Malaysia. These different ethnic groups have also created their own schools, placing importance on their own languages and implicit culture. In addition, international schools were built where syllabus from abroad (UK, US or Singapore) were taught. It is also worth noting that Malaysia is a member of the Commonwealth of Nations. This meant that British influence has been prolific, demonstrated by the use of English language, the side of the road we drive on, the use of the common law legal system, to the presence of Marmite in our households.

I started my education in a Chinese school where I learnt Mandarin as the primary language, then moved to a Malay school although English was predominantly spoken in this school. Whilst I have categorised schools in terms of language, this is inseparable from the religion and the traditions that surround these languages. There is more emphasis on my 'religion of origin' (i.e. the religion I was born with), attending religious classes were mandatory, where previously in the Chinese school, it was never required. I felt I had to display more adherence to the culture and religion, such as by participating in prayers and greeting others in Arabic.

Despite this, cultural assimilation at a societal level is minimal, mainly driven by governmental policies and structure designed to favour Malays who are often poorer and live in rural areas to the dissatisfaction of other ethnic groups who feel alienated and possess higher economic and social powers. The intention is to protect the privilege of 'bumiputera'. Such policies have not abated the racial hatred and gulf that has had a long history between the main ethnic groups, and began during the British colonisation when immigration was encouraged for labour and to expand the economy.

This was exemplified in a racial riot on 13 May 1969. Official figures numbered the death toll at around 200, but unofficial and realistic estimates were five or ten times that figure (Mehmet, 1974). Though the event occurred 49 years ago, it is still fresh in the memory of the living generation, certainly, in my family's mind. This opens up an intergenerational trauma that … Malaysia generally projects a peaceful image and a superficial harmony, yet in reality, there is widespread discrimination in housing, finance, judicial and education systems.

To the UK

Sending one's child abroad for further education was not uncommon. Education is important for Malaysian parents and they make financial sacrifice to ensure that their children receive the best education. In a survey, it was found that Australia (67 per cent) was the most popular choice, followed by UK (38 per cent) and United States (24 per cent) (Suresh Ram, 2017). At fifteen, I arrived at a school which had many international students predominantly from China, followed by Malaysia, Singapore or Vietnam, and other East Asian countries. Being away from home, I enjoyed and relished in the freedom this gave me. It also never felt too foreign as my fellow schoolmates broadly shared a similar culture to myself. Dutifully, I was focused on my education, graduated from college, and embarked on an undergraduate degree. Throughout this period, I rarely had any negative experience of being 'the other' with my peer group who mainly comprised of East Asians, except a few comments occasionally from British strangers telling me to 'go back to my country'. I recalled my first felt experience of being 'different' when a course mate of mine during a small group project commented in an astounded way 'why are there so many international people here?!' It was a strange feeling, but I shrugged it off at that time. I also recalled when choosing my course modules with my director of studies, I told her that in my culture, I am not accustomed to being controversial, therefore politics would not be suitable for me. All these were signs that I held and followed a cultural assumption, but not to a strong degree of awareness.

The first time I was required to reflect deeply on my identity was during my training in counselling psychology. My confusion on my identity can be exemplified by the filling in of an equality and diversity monitoring form, I used to think that I am a 'British Asian' and would tick this. However, over the years, the category 'Chinese' appeared, sometimes under 'Asian', at other times it was a standalone category separate from 'Asian'. As Chinese was the closest ethnicity for me on this form, I supposed this was my next best option, but still, I was very confused. I asked some of my friends who were white British, and they explained that 'British Asians' tend to be used to refer to people from the region of India, Pakistan or Bangladesh. So, as I am of a mixed ethnic background of Malay and Chinese, which category do I fall under? The wider literature especially from the US tend to refer to Asians as those from China, Korea and Japan. I have come to be accustomed with and certainly relate more to this terminology. This led me to wonder if there were cultural differences in how these terminologies are decided. It certainly makes the water murkier.

If you saw me, you may immediately think that I am Chinese, but my name may indicate that I am a Malay/Muslim. Psychotherapeutically, this has an impact; I recalled one of my psychodynamic lecturers saying that the process of therapy starts when the client receives the appointment letter with your name on it. Clients begin to imagine how their therapist (and vice versa) would be like and projects their anxieties onto this. An example that came to mind was when I was due to start therapy with a war veteran who had participated in tours in Iraq and Afghanistan. After receiving the appointment letter, he phoned up requesting for a different psychologist as he was afraid of offending me with what he might bring to therapy and wanted to 'protect me'. I was interested in working through this with the client, and with the little I knew about him from the assessment session, I wondered if 'protecting others' is one of his primary relational patterns, especially considering his previous occupation. However, for various reasons my supervisor and myself decided that he was best placed to be seen by another psychologist.

According to the Malaysian Constitution, every person has the right to profess and to practice his or her religion. The Constitution also stipulates that Islam is the religion of the country but other religion may be practiced in peace and harmony. The religious conversion of Muslims lies within the jurisdiction of Islamic courts. Indeed, Malaysia has a dual system of law, and some matters for those who are Muslims are governed by Syariah law and the Syariah Court. In practice, conversion from Islam is fraught with difficulties, barriers and controversy and many who have converted to other religions choose to lead double lives hiding their new faith from the community. However, this poses a problem when matters such as marriage and inheritance come into play which are governed by Syariah law (Pressly, 2006). Therefore, one who may not self-identify as Muslim would have no choice in such legal matters. For example, in inheritance, the Malaysian shariah law stipulates that they can only bequeath in their will one third of their assets to whoever they want, including non-Muslim family members (Noordin et al., 2012).

As my father was a Muslim, officially I am one too. I joined religious classes and learnt these texts growing up. However, of stronger influence is my mother's side of the family, we celebrated Chinese customs and was brought up in Confucian principles. Confucian teachings are rooted in the ethical system of jen (humaneness), yi (righteousness) and li (rules of propriety). Tsai (2005) wrote that 'Confucius' emphasis on the filial piety, family values, the "love of gradation", altruism of people, and the "role specified relation-oriented ethics", hence tends to grant "beneficence" a favourable position that diminishes the respect for individual rights and autonomy' (p.159). Broadly, this is interpreted to show reserve and restrain in public display of emotions and opinions. Being overly expressive and opinionated is a sign of disrespect and weak self-control. It is worth noting that, this does not mean that one is not capable of expressing emotions or opinions. The underlying principle is the cultivation of harmony in interpersonal relationships, and this is primary to that of individual needs. However, in my opinion, these principles which are cultivated from a young age, if left unchecked could create a sense of dissociation, leading to emotional and psychological distancing from others. One might find themselves unable to access or adequately express their feelings as they may have never been encouraged to speak about them. So rather than being emotionally restrained, they are emotionally blank. This has certainly been something I grappled with, more so in the past, I had a rational, problem solving, and outcome focused approach in general. I had felt unable to reflect on my own thoughts or beliefs in the moment, and adequately express what I think or feel when asked about something. When I was at a placement in a Dialectical Behavioural Therapy service and co-facilitating the skills group, I found it very helpful to learn to name and discover nuances of emotions, to practice mindfulness and gain more awareness of my cognitive processes, and to learn that actually these are skills that could be acquired.

Perception of mental health and therapy

Psychiatric treatment and mental health therapeutic support took the form of institutions originated from British administration at that time. Since then, mental health system in Malaysia has seen some reforms including the passing of the Mental Health Act (2001) that sets out policy and guidelines for mental health services, increase in establishments of community psychosocial support and increase in training of allied mental health professionals. Nonetheless, more work remains to be done on raising public awareness of mental health as cultural and traditional practices are still followed by Malaysians, which hinders normalisation of distressing experiences. Psychiatric assessment may only be sought as a last resort, by which point the individuals' presentation becomes severe and enduring. Interestingly, Haque (2005) also identified that psychiatrists in Malaysia are reliant on their Western training and fail to take into account cultural factors. In addition to that, mental health professionals were not as well publicly perceived a career as other jobs might be as this area suffers from poor image in general. I certainly recalled when I told my extended family members some years ago at a wedding about my training, they laughed and said 'You sure? It takes a crazy person to know another crazy person'.

Haque (2005) posited that mental health can be considered a reflection of the person's healthy and positive behaviours in relation to a culture. Certainly, those of us who are involved in the psychopathology and assessment of certain mental health disorders such as personality disorder or schizophrenia know that it is imperative that these are interpreted in light of the individual's culture.

Spiritual, religious and cultural factors related to ethnicity play a vital part in the perception of mental health in Malaysia. There is also a general tendency to interpret psychological problems in physical terms. Malays who tend to follow the religion of Islam might seek help for psychological problems from traditional healers called bomohs or pawing who use mantras and traditional ingredients to rid the person of whatever may have taken over the individuals' body such as an unwelcomed spirit, witchcraft or black magic. One might be made susceptible to these invasions, due to a loss of inner strength (semangat), mental stress and religious immorality (Razali, Khan and Hasanah, 2005). There is a higher tendency to reject the concepts of mental illness or issues, as it is believed that these stem from supernatural activities (Ng, 1997). Interestingly, due to this, the Malays are generally more supportive of those who suffer from mental health problems. It has been observed and to be noted though that Malaysian Malays beliefs about mental illness do not correspond to those of Islam which is their primary religion. This shows that the influence of one's cultural beliefs may be different from religious ones; however, this could also be due to a difference in whether individuals are from rural or urban backgrounds. In rural areas, one is generally left alone whereas in urban areas, they are avoided by those around them (Hanafiah and Bortel, 2015).

In Hinduism, mental health is attributed to one's diet, relationship with deities, teachers and the Brahmins (Haque, 2005; Razali et al., 1996). Less is known about their perception and help seeking attitude compared to Malays and Chinese.

Chinese attribute good physical and mental health to the emotional state of a person. A mentally healthy person is signified by good interpersonal skills, controlling emotions and rational thinking (Palmer, 2015). Illnesses are perceived to have occurred when unbalanced emotions are expressed. Self-worth is measured and respects from others are obtained from material achievements one brings to their family. This could be in the form of a socially desirable occupation, level of education achieved, and financial status. Mental health problems are perceived as shameful and disclosure are avoided to protect the family from 'losing face' (shamed). They might even be shunned from their family members and friends, who may not want to be responsible for the perceived unpredictability in behaviour of someone labelled with mental illness specifically those diagnosed with Schizophrenia, Bipolar Disorder and Depression. Participants, who were surveyed in a study, reported that they believe the general public thought they had bad genes and psychological weaknesses that attributed to their conditions (Hanafiah & Bortel, 2015). It appears that the perception towards mental health of Malaysian Chinese follows closely to that of other Asian countries that broadly follow Confucian's societal principles, with dominant feelings of shame, guilt and honour.

These perceptions may have a bearing in terms of help and therapy seeking which is best encapsulated by the following personal example. The family of a Malaysian I knew who had Christian beliefs, and would self-identify as Malaysian Chinese chose to seek the help of a traditional healer or bomoh rather than psychiatric help for a breakdown. This is perhaps due to the stigma surrounding mental health and thus an externalisation of factors (possessed by spirits in this case) rather than examination of psychological processes. When the spirits are expelled from the body, the person is thus considered healed, personal and systemic circumstances were never examined.

Degree of acculturation and enculturation

In the UK, there is generally less societal stigma with accessing and receiving mental health support compared to Malaysia. There are also active efforts to dispel marginalisation and propel improvement of mental health services such as the Five Year Forward View for Mental Health strategy (NHS England, 2016). Therefore, in theory, this should encourage Malaysians residing in the UK to access help. However, as previously illustrated, it appears that the reaction from immediate community such as friends and family play a crucial role in facilitating this process. Nonetheless, on an individual level, for Malaysians predominantly from urban areas, British influences, economic progress and the use of internet has resulted in varying levels of Western values incorporated into their personal concepts. This will in turn impact on their perception of mental health and therapy seeking behaviour independent of the community especially if they are far away from home residing in the UK without familial presence. Perhaps the distance also provides relief from being answerable to the dominant discourses in Malaysian society and of immediate family.

Even if this barrier is surmounted, navigating through a predominantly individualistic culture which favours extraversion, assertiveness, autonomy, and where the need for privacy is looser (Triandis, 2001) could disrupt the psychological equilibrium of someone from a collectivist culture. They would undergo a complex interplay between accepting and rejecting values from their home and the dominant culture across different life domains such as work, school, family, friends and relationships. Acculturation as it is known refers to 'level of involvement in the culture of origin and the dominant culture' and enculturation refers to the 'process of adaptation and retention of one's indigenous culture, values, ideas and concepts' (Kim, 2015). I understood this at an experiential level during my doctoral training, where I started to reflect deeply on my culture of origin and sought to understand this dominant culture, I am in which felt quite polarising at times. It was a disarming experience as up until that point, I have been quite involved with my own community of friends who shared similar background to me. It also made me think more about which values to retain and perhaps more accurately, in which domains I retain them.

This process started when things I never saw as a barrier in interpersonal relationships such as emotional restrain, problem solving, deference to authority figures and humility was suddenly causing me significant amount of discomforts and 'trouble' at my placements. Up until that point, I have never been someone that says 'hello', or asked questions such as 'how are you?' which for me felt ingenuine when the answer one typically expects is 'I'm fine'. For me, nodding and exchanging glances was sufficient as a 'hello'. This was highlighted to me by my then clinical supervisor who commented that others have noticed that I do not greet others. I was further flustered by questions such as 'how do you feel about this client?'; I did not understand how my feelings were important in carrying out therapy and these lines of questioning as such felt intrusive and as though I was 'doing the wrong thing'. Explaining what I think I have done well also felt like a lack of humility on my part but perceived as a lack of self-confidence from the 'other'. The collaborative stance that my supervisor employed also felt like a lack of guidance, yet I did not feel I could let him know. I thought 'how could I possibly teach someone more experienced and older (thus the assumption of wiser person) than me how to do his job'. In my mind, I saw his role as a 'teacher' and 'mentor'. This subsequently triggered other things such as a sense of not being able to meet others and my expectations. I felt like a failure as I mulled over – 'Why do I keep getting this wrong?' but confused as to 'what am I getting wrong?'. These experiences hit my self-identity and worth so hard at that time that I remembered one day, I was frozen in dejection. I felt so drained that I was not able to feed myself and had to rely on my partner to literally feed me (which if we psychoanalyse might reveal subconscious needs!). Looking back, I was confused, angry, conflicted, upset and felt grossly misunderstood although unable to find the words to explain this nor able to understand what I was going through.

Since then, I began to realise that I made changes and operate differently in separate domains. At work, I employ a more assertive, outgoing, emotionally expressive self. However, when I am with people from my culture especially with those who are less familiar, these can be perceived as disrespectful and therefore I am more mindful of the questions I ask and the opinions I express. In my recent personal relationship, I have incorporated more autonomy and emotional expressiveness, although retained the sense of duty, family integrity and filial piety in my relationship to my parents. After more than a decade of being in the UK, I see myself as a first-generation immigrant, who although did not make a choice to come here initially, has decided to move here due to socio-cultural values and economic prospects. This feels more empowering than if the immigration was necessary for other reasons.

Applying these to therapeutic practice

This article is by no means exhaustive, I am aware there are other avenues that could be further explored. Nonetheless, drawing everything together so far, below are some suggestions when working with Malaysians in the UK, and those who share similar background as Malaysia's demographics. In line with the principles underpinning counselling psychology, the following prioritises understanding the subjective experience and developmental concepts of the client as well as reflecting on the interpersonal dynamics between the psychologist and client. In my opinion, the latter is specifically important as cultural adaptation is a relational experience (Douglas et al., 2016).

- Assess religion at birth and growing up, traditions and cultures that were followed within the family and current self-identified religion and ethnic culture.
- How is one with their religion, ethnic and cultural background perceived in their home country? How does one think they are perceived in the UK? What impact does this have on their identity and sense of self?
- How did they perceive their move to the UK? Did they have a choice? If not, what are their thoughts about the future residency and how does this impact on level of acculturation.
- Degree of acculturation, considering that there is a possibility that the level of acculturation might be different across different life domains.
- Able to tolerate that the client might view the therapist as 'the other' thus feeling unable to explore the above in the session, perhaps thinking that you are not interested or that perhaps it is not important.
- Alternatively, the therapist might be perceived as an ally, especially if there is ethnic matching or knowing that the therapist has been a resident or visitor in their own country. This might lead to an assumption that the therapist knows the depth of what they are referring to.
- If they report difficulties due to cultural mismatch, consider emphatically with the client how these were misperceived by others, and what steps they could take to either educate or adapt. The latter would have to be explored tentatively and done sensitively considering the client's overall goals and values across various life domains.
- What does the client need at this moment to build a therapeutic rapport and working alliance? Is being directive and solution focused conducive at present or insight orientated, emotion focused exploratory work appropriate. Develop caution against labelling what belongs to cultural upbringing as 'defence mechanisms'. Concepts that are perceived in that culture as a virtue should be respected even if it does not fit with yours. For instance, distinguish between presentations such as humility or reserve and lack of assertiveness.
- On a similar note, encourage clients to consider their interpretation of cultural concepts which may have led to unhelpful ways of reacting in situations. For instance, mistaking humility with not standing up for oneself when the situation requires it.

Summary

It is clear that even within the collectivist culture of Malaysia, there are varying perceptions on mental health and therapy depending on religious, traditional and ethnic backgrounds. In addition to that, those who are currently residing in the UK, will face the additional complex interplay between adapting to and retaining features of their home culture to the dominant individualistic culture. Holding a curious stance in relation to religion, ethnicity and traditions and respecting one's cultural values are cornerstones to fostering a relational therapeutic space.

Dr Masrita Ishaq
Counselling Psychologist

References

Current Population Estimates, Malaysia 2016–2017. Department of Statistics Malaysia, Official Portal. Retrieved on 30th October 2018 at https://www.dosm.gov.my/v1/index.php?r=column/cthemeByCat&cat=155&bul_id=a1d1UTFZazd5ajJiRWFHNDduOXFFQT09&menu_id=L0pheU43NWJwRWVSZklWdzQ4TlhUUT09

Douglas, B., Woolfe, R., Strawbridge, S., Kasket, E. & Galbraith, V. (Eds.) (2016). *The handbook of counselling psychology 4th edition.* London: Sage.

Haque, A. (2005). Mental health concepts and program development in Malaysia. *Journal of Mental Health, 14*(2), 183–195.

Ibrahim, A. (2005, August 16) Embrace English as "Our" Language. *New Straits Times,* p.4

Kim, L. (2015) Psychotherapy with Asian clients: An exploratory study of the perspectives of East Asian clinicians (unpublished doctoral dissertation). Rutgers, the state university of new jersey, New Jersey.

Mehmet, O. (1974) Race riots in Malaysia. *Salient Victoria University Student Newspaper 37* (15), pp.10–11.

Ng, C.H. (1997) The stigma of mental illness in Asian cultures. *Australian and New Zealand Journal of Psychiatry, 31,* 382–390.

NHS England (2016). Five Year Forward View for Mental Health. Retrieved 11 April 2019 from https://www.england.nhs.uk/wp-content/uploads/2016/02/Mental-Health-Taskforce-FYFV-final.pdf

Noordin, N., Shuib, A., Zainol, M.S. & Mohamed Adil, M.A. (2012) Review on issues and challenges in Islamic inheritance distribution in Malaysia. *OIDA International Journal of Sustainable Development 03:12,* 27–38.

Suresh Ram, B. (2017, August 11) Parents in Malaysia spend an average of RM110,000 on their child's education. *New Straits Times.* Retrieved from https://www.nst.com.my/news/nation/2017/08/266529/parents-malaysia-spend-average-rm110000-their-childs-education

Palmer, B.B. (2015) Concepts of mental health in Malaysia. *International Journal of Mental Health in Malaysia, 44*(3), 253–258.

Pillai, S. (2008) Speaking English the Malaysia way – correct or not? An examination of the give and take between local varieties and the expectations of classroom English. *English Today 96, Vol 24* (4). Cambridge University Press.

Pressly, L. (2006, November 15) Life as a secret Christian Convert. Retrieved from http://news.bbc.co.uk/1/hi/programmes/crossing_continents/6150340.stm

Razali, S.M., Khan, U.A. & Hasanah, C.I. (1996) Belief in supernatural causes of mental illness among Malay patients: impact on treatment. *Acta Psychiatrica Scandinavica 94,* 229–233.

Reid, A. & Spotswood, R.D. (1988–1993). *Southeast Asia in the age of commerce, 1450–1680.* New Haven: Yale University Press.

Triandis, H.C. (2001) Individualism and collectivism: Past, present and future. In D. Matsumoto (Ed.) *Handbook of culture and psychology.* New York: Oxford University.

Tsai, D.F. (2005) The bioethical principles and Confucius moral philosophy. *Journal of Medical Ethics 31,* 159–163.

'Mind The Gap': Services for all

Zenobia Nadirshaw

The World Health Organisation defines Learning disabilities/Intellectual difficulties as when a person has a:
- Significant impairment of intellectual function.
- Significant impairment of adaptive/social functioning.
- Age of onset before adulthood (18 years).

In general usage this definition describes a group of people with significant developmental delay that – results in arrested or incomplete achievement – in the 'normal' milestones of human development. These milestones relate to intellectual, emotional, spiritual and social aspects of development. Significant delays in a number of these areas could lead to a person being identified as having an Intellectual Disability (ID). Other terms such as learning difficulty, mentally impaired, imbecile, idiot, educationally subnormal, uneducable, mentally retarded have been used. Thankfully with the different theoretical approaches to understanding this condition (psychological, sociological, medical and anthropological) these terms no longer perceive a person with intellectual difficulties as a sick person (medical perspective). It is well known that ID is a social construct, the presence of which may be difficult to determine in the absence of ID associated syndrome, or a significant history of developmental delay, or educational history. Among black and minority ethnic communities, the language barriers, lack of education and healthcare opportunities in their country of origin and incomplete or unsubstantiated histories make assessment especially complicated (Royal College of Psychiatrists, 2011).

Gates & Wilberforce (2004) describe the incidence and prevalence of ID as problematic due to the difficulties in detecting such disability at birth – in that there may be no physical manifestation of the disability at birth until delays in development manifest themselves. With reference to prevalence, this is concerned with the estimation of the number of people with a condition, disorder or disease as a proportion of the general population. If one sees intelligence quotient (IQ) as an indicator of ID, then it is calculated that 2 to 3 per cent of the population have an IQ below 70 on the normal distribution curve of intelligence. Gates and Wilberforce (2004) stated that the prevalence of moderate and severe ID is approximately 3 to 4 persons per 1000 of the general population. While Grant (1985) identified 3.7 per 1000 population for people with severe and moderate ID.

The Department of Health has suggested that mild ID is quite common with prevalence being estimated to be in the region of 20 persons per 1000 of the general population. In the UK, it has been further calculated that of the 3 to 4 persons with severe or profound ID have multiple disabilities as well as behavioural difficulties. For a greater understanding of the incidence of prevalence of ID, the reader is referred to Chapter 1, 'The Nature of Learning Disability' by Gates and Wilberforce (2004).

Britain is a multi-ethnic, multicultural society with nearly 14 per cent of the English and Welsh population coming from Black and minority ethnic (BME) communities, with a concentration in the London and inner city areas. Evidence on the prevalence of ID in BME communities is not consistent. Conceptual and practical difficulties with the definition of ID make prevalence data across ethnic groups and from communities around the world difficult to establish.

Nadirshaw (1997) alerts to the double discrimination and double disadvantage the people with learning disabilities from BME backgrounds experience. She warns of the 'victim blaming' as well as the colour-blind approach within the service system by the powerful professionals who do not acknowledge the fact that the mental health and psychological needs are affected by social and political stances – leading to people of a BME background being viewed – and treated as of less value than their white counterparts, resulting in the denial of a positive black racial and cultural identity.

The Normalisation Principle which is also referred to as 'social role valorisation' (Wolfensberger, 1983) has been based on the belief that people with ID should be socially accepted and valued with the same right as other non-disabled people, to live in mainstream society as valued respected citizens. Potentially, normalisation and social role valorisation principles are a force for good. However, they make certain blanket assumptions about what are 'normal' or 'valued' in society. The needs, wants or wishes of white majority of people are, on the whole, considered 'normal' or 'valued' whilst the needs of BME clients tends to be ignored. Despite government legalisation and the Race Relations (Amendment) Act 2000, there are questions that need to be asked when working with difference and the double discrimination that comes about in service ideology, service provision and service delivery (Nadirshaw, 1997). The Act sets out the key areas of discrimination as direct and indirect discrimination. The Act also emphasises the general duty of all National Health Service (NHS) organisations to promote Race Equality by eliminating unlawful racial discrimination.

Mental health of people with ID

Between 25 per cent and 40 per cent of people with ID, also experience some form of mental health difficulty (Mental Health Foundation, 2011). Mental Health Foundation in 2011 estimate that 1.5 million people in the UK have an ID – this includes 905,000 adults aged 18+ and 286,000 children. It is well known that people with ID are more likely to experience physical and mental health problems with 25 to 40 per cent experiencing some form of mental health problem. Laura A. Huges – McCormack et al. (2017) study of people with ID in England and Scotland found 12.8 per cent children, 23.4 per cent adults and 27.2 per cent older adults had mental health conditions compared to 0.3 per cent, 5.3 per cent and 4.5 per cent of the general population. Costello & Bouras (2006) state that despite the fact that people with ID face an increased vulnerability to developing mental health problems, there is a lack of agreement about the most appropriate form of assessment.

People with ID suffer from mental health problems as well as being vulnerable to exploitation. Mental health problems in people with ID have largely been neglected, with widespread under-diagnoses and under-reporting of mental health conditions.

The Royal College of Psychiatrists (2004) identifies several reasons for this. One such reason is the general belief that people with problems and the behavioural difficulties as shown by this group, is attributed to their ID. Fortunately, there is now a belief that these people do experience mental ill health, just as the general population do, but they are the most vulnerable in society (Smiley, 2004).

Life events similar to those of the general population can also affect people with ID. Adults with ID, experience at least as many life events and are as vulnerable as those adults without ID but suffer from affective or neurotic disorder. There is evidence that people from minority ethnic communities are more likely to be diagnosed with psychiatric illness, especially psychosis, than the white Caucasian population.

The Foundation for People with ID identifies the following mental health disorders and states in percentage terms the prevalence rates:

Disorder	Rates
Schizophrenia	3%
Bipolar affective disorder	1.5%
Depression	4%
Generalised anxiety disorder	6%
Specific phobia	6%
Agoraphobia	1.5%
Obsessive–compulsive disorder	2.5%
Dementia at age 65 years and over	20%
Autism	7%
Severe problem behaviour	10%–15%

Estimated prevalence rates from population based studies of adults with ID

People with ID suffer from mental health difficulties and are vulnerable to risk of psychotic disorders as the general population with additional and specific factors of brain damage, epilepsy, repeated loss or separation, communication difficulties, poor coping mechanisms leading to decreased self-esteem, impaired social and family relationships and other psychological factors. Management of treatment of mental health include the use of pharmacological treatment, electroconvulsive therapy (ECT), psychological treatment and other alternative treatments.

The Mental Health of Children and Adolescents with Learning Disabilities in Britain: a publication funded by the Foundation for People with Learning Disabilities (Emerson & Hatton, 2007) highlights that children with learning disabilities are at a greater risk of mental ill health and developing mental health problems as compared with their peers.

The lack of social services and interpreting services coupled with social attitudes of discrimination at the point of delivery appear to be the major obstacles to service users. In addition, emotional and psychological distress may not be recognised by GPs who often identify somatic problems with this group.

There is responsibility in the helping professions to ensure that they are equipped to work within an equal opportunity perspective that will prepare them to work in a multi-racial, multicultural context. Improving access to psychotherapy (IAPT) is an NHS initiative to improve the psychological health care of people living in England. This should include people with ID coming from BAME backgrounds too.

The helping professional needs to provide a service that is diverse, clinically appropriate and culturally sound in today's Britain. They must accept this responsibility, work towards building a more inclusive society, and respond by having the appropriate understanding of problems faced by an invisible segment of British society, whose need for psychological services and input may be expressed differently. Theoretical frameworks for psychotherapeutic practice must move away from dealing with concepts that are central to middle-class white populations and provide teaching and training about population that is culturally and ethnically diverse. Widespread silence and indifference is preventing the problem from getting the attention it deserves.

Different psychological interventions need to be offered and which need to be adapted to ensure appropriateness of their use for this group of people. Different forms of therapy within individual, group and family work with the following adaptations need to be provided. The latter might include keeping verbal and written language as simple as possible, the use of non-verbal techniques, such as drawing, use of Makaton sign language, respect for the person's ability to concentrate and include (or not include) the person's support network – including support staff and/or the joint community learning disability team members (viz. community nurses, language therapist), advocates and qualified interpreters. Working with a person with ID from a BME background may take a longer time to develop a culturally appropriate assessment and intervention plan due to their lack of being offered counselling or psychotherapy input in the past. It is important that primary care team members – including GPs recognise the need for psychological intervention for this group rather than prescribing medication for their so-called 'challenging' behaviours. Links with the different voluntary sectors including the black voluntary sector is also highly recommended.

There are significant barriers to psychotherapy for people with ID (Royal College of Psychiatrists, 2004). A person with ID may be afraid to talk to their GP when they are physically ill or emotionally distressed for fear of being labelled a trouble-maker. There is an apparent widespread lack of understanding between professionals and people with ID. The author highlights the fact that psychotherapists remain reluctant to engage with people with ID, citing inappropriate supervision and a lack of confidence as the reasons for this. Helping professionals believe that psychological therapies is better reserved for people with more cognitive abilities with therapeutic 'disdain' becoming more 'institutionalised' and being perceived as unrewarding. However, Taylor, Lyndsay and Willner (2008) hold a different viewpoint.

In the author's view, the attitude towards people with ID from BME communities, the interpersonal skills and ability to show genuine empathy, concern, and respect that is meaningful to the client, far outweighs the type of therapy used.

Meaningful contact leading to a positive relationship between the helping professional and the BME client with ID goes a long way to achieving a positive outcome.

Working within an anti-oppressive, proactive relationship, assessing the quality of the client's relationship with the therapist leads to a cooperative therapeutic alliance in which the client develops confidence in the therapist with feelings of security arising from the constructive, genuinely compassionate approach that should be adopted toward the client. The helping professional's support to the status quo and being socialised to work within the system and rarely challenging the negative racist stereotype needs to be identified and worked through so that a person with an ID from a BME community will achieve his or her potential.

Wilberforce (2004) identifies common factors among the psychological approaches – irrespective of the approach/intervention used. They are:

- The relationship between client and the therapist.
- The working alliance between client and therapist.
- The support provided to, and reassuring manner shown to the client.
- The insight that is developed in the client following therapeutic work.
- The reinforcement of healthy and adaptive change in the client.

From a psychoanalytical perspective, Sinason (1992) suggested that a person with ID may adopt secondary handicaps, such as compliant exaggeration of the original handicap to keep others happy, and appearing submissive, acquiescent, and eager to please, as a defence against their stigmatised identity.

For children and young people, the prevalence rate of a diagnosable psychiatric disorder is 36 per cent, compared with 8 per cent of those who do not have an ID. These young people are also 33 times more likely to be on the autistic spectrum and are much more likely than others to have emotional and conduct disorders.

Children and young people with ID are much more likely than others to live in poverty, to have few friends and to have additional long-term health problems and disabilities such as epilepsy and sensory impairments. All these factors are positively associated with mental health problems. All of us experience challenges around our emotional wellbeing at some stage in our lives, with one in four (www.who.int/whr/2001/media_centre/press_release/en/) of us experiencing a problem with our mental health in any one year. Children and adults with ID and other forms of disabilities are not exempt from this.

People with ID demonstrate the complete spectrum of mental health problems, with higher prevalence than found in those without ID (Source: RCP 2004, Intellectual disabilities). For example, the prevalence of dementia is much higher amongst older adults with ID compared to the general population (21.6 per cent vs 5.7 per cent, aged 65+) (Cooper, 1997a). People with Down's Syndrome are at particularly high risk of developing dementia, with an age of onset 30 to 40 years younger than the general population (Mozes, 2018). Prevalence rates for schizophrenia in people with ID are approximately three times greater than for the general population —3%= per cent vs 1 per cent (Doody et al., 1998).

Reported prevalence rates for anxiety and depression amongst people with ID vary widely but are generally reported to be at least as prevalent as the general population (Stavrakaki, 1999), and higher amongst people with Down's Syndrome (Collacott et al., 1998).

Challenging behaviours (aggression, destruction, self-injury and others) are shown by 10 to 15 per cent of people with ID, with age-specific prevalence peaking between ages 20 and 49 (Emerson et al., 2001) (Sources taken from Key Highlights of Research Evidence on the Health of People with Learning [Intellectual] Disabilities).

Emerson and Hatton (2007) report that 36 per cent of children and young people with ID will have a mental health problem, compared with 8 per cent of non-ID children.

The risk factors that contribute are usually a mix of those within the child (IQ, genetic influences, physical illness and communication difficulties) and from external sources (socio-economic disadvantage, discrimination, loss and family breakdown).

People with ID and their Human Rights

They have the right:

- To access an inclusive education – irrespective of their background or country of birth. It is about the right to receive quality education and ensuring all their needs are met.
- To access advocates and the different types of advocacy offered to this group of people.
- To access evidence based therapeutic interventions, which increase motivation and self-image.
- To create opportunities to visit their country of birth and to use all the additional facilities in the community.
- To receive appropriate care packages which take a holistic perspective and incorporate aspects of culture, ethnicity and inclusivity.
- To work with trained staff who have received training in diversity, inclusivity and equal opportunities and staff who are competent working with and removing barriers caused by poverty, cultural and conscious/unconscious bias towards people with ID.
- To social, physical mental and emotional wellbeing by being out and about in their community/communities.
- To a process of redirection of professionals and other carers, involving professional skills into the context of their cultural and community needs, practicing these new skills within the community environment and building new activities and self-esteem.
- To develop skills which confront environmental barriers which prevent people with ID to live ordinary lives.
- To a more collaborative and cooperative partnership within services with the individual client rather than an authoritarian and hierarchical one.
- To move away from a medical model to a social model with a stronger focus on ability rather than disability and to use new found skills. In the community as well as mixed with all the members of the community and local neighbourhood.
- To the provision of culturally appropriate food (e.g. halal food), if necessary and appropriate culturally relevant activities – including celebrating special cultural events/days for example Diwali (the Hindu new year), visits to religious temples and adherences to fasting rituals.

- To have access to appropriate therapeutic interventions and the development of a sound therapeutic alliance (Nadirshaw, 2014).
- To ensure services and families enable the person with ID meet with other people to develop emotional and social relationships and network. Service providers to get to know the person's friends from school and college via the person centred planning approach and create opportunities to foster friendships and interests.
- To offer complementary therapies in the form of massage, aromatherapy, reflexology, relaxation, mindfulness should also be considered. Unfortunately, at the present moment, the information is relatively limited although therapeutic benefits have been acknowledged (Vickers, 1994, 1997).
- To actively work with independent organisations, voluntary organisations, campaigning organisations, education, employment, health, and social service agencies with a view that individual needs are met in a coordinated manner.
- To get Primary Care Services and GP services to actively monitor the health care for people with ID and offer guidance on appropriate exercise and eating habits to avoid risks of heart diseases.
- To get all staff trained in developing cultural appropriate goals and standards for black and ethnic minority people and to develop confidence in questioning the principles of normalisation and their interpretations and the Anglo Saxon values inherent in them.

Key points: Therapy for people with ID coming from BME Communities

People with ID have mental health problems, which need to be addressed in an appropriate manner in therapeutic work. People with ID from BME are less likely to have access to or be referred to appropriate multicultural or transcultural services. People with ID from BME backgrounds and their specific needs remain invisible to the statutory service sector, which still maintains a colour-blind approach. Services and service providers continue to perpetuate the ideology of 'all needs are the same' with the idea that culture is a problem not the services.

The systematic maintenance of a colour-blind approach in therapeutic practice where 'one size fits all' needs to be avoided completely. Formal recognition of the diverse and varied needs of this group needs to be addressed, for example, acknowledging mental health problems with this population, the different languages and words used to communicate emotional distress, the cultural variations of how distressed mental ill health and wellbeing are expressed.

The perspective of anti-oppressive and anti-discriminative practice needs to be advocated and learned by psychotherapists, counsellors and psychologists. To note the legal considerations contained within the range of government acts, policy laws and practices versus the basic human rights and obligations contained within an anti-oppressive practice (British Psychological Society, 2016).

Emphasis is on the psychotherapist, counsellors, psychologists to move away from the conditioned Eurocentric and ethnocentric perspective of the individual to the real understanding of the lack of autonomy, capacity, and the social position of the BME ID client in society. Safety, trust, respect and collaboration are some of the positive features that constitute therapeutic alliance, which then leads to positive outcomes.

Psychological/psychotherapeutic practice

Different psychological interventions exist (Beail, 2016). The helping professionals need to make available appropriate psychological and other therapeutic interventions for emotional and other behavioural problems using materials which are familiar to ID clients and particularly to ID clients from BME backgrounds. The use of appropriate additional cues (signs, pictures, symbols, videos to assist in communication with a person with ID and their carer whose first language is not English).

Psychological treatment in the form of cognitive behavioural therapy, psychodynamic therapy, supportive psychotherapy that uses a range of ways to communicate with people with ID should be used. For example, music therapy, appropriate words which are meaningful in the person's culture, assisting the person with hearing impairments, appropriate facial expression, use of soap operas and the actor's emotional expression as identification of emotional distress and of mental health. The principle of gaining an accurate picture of the person's comprehension of language and finding appropriate ways to communicate is one of the basic ethical principles in the therapeutic work with people with ID. The helping professional needs to fully understand and develop the appropriate skills accordingly.

Ethical practice in ID

Parents commonly wonder and ask how they can know whether their child has an ID. While there is no one sign that shows a person has these challenges, educational and clinical professionals look for a noticeable difference between how well a child does in school and how well the child can do given their assessed intelligence or ability? There are many signs that may indicate that a child has an ID, and many of these signs become apparent in elementary school, when a child is increasingly required to demonstrate learning skills and knowledge. If a child displays multiple difficulties, then parents and teachers may consider the possibility that the child has an ID. The following is a list of questions (most here specific to elementary grades but may be applicable for adolescents and adults) that parents can ask a teacher in determining the probability of such a disability.

- Does my child have trouble learning the alphabet, rhyming words, or connecting letters to their sounds?
- Does my child have difficulties for his/her age sounding out and decoding words and letter combinations?
- Does my child have trouble remembering the sounds that letters make or hearing slight differences between words?
- Is my child often mispronouncing words or often using a wrong word that sounds similar?
- Is my child making many mistakes when reading aloud, and does he or she repeat and pause often when reading orally?
- Is my child having difficulty understanding what he or she reads?
- Is my child having difficulty with spelling?
- Does my child have very poor handwriting, or does he or she hold a pencil awkwardly for his or her age?
- Is my child having difficulties understanding and using fundamental rules of grammar, syntax, and punctuation when writing?

- Is my child showing great difficulties expressing ideas in writing?
- Is my child having difficulties with organising his or her thoughts when attempting to write organisationally?
- Does my child appear to have difficulties following verbal directions?
- Does my child appear to have difficulties making him or herself understood by using language; for instance, is he or she able to verbalise feelings, frustrations, etc., at a developmentally appropriate level?
- Does my child appear to have a limited developing vocabulary for his or her age?
- Does my child appear to have trouble organising what he or she wants to say at a developmentally appropriate level?
- Does my child appear often unable to think of the word he or she needs when speaking or writing?
- Does my child appear to have trouble understanding jokes, comic strips, stories, and sarcasm at a developmentally appropriate level?
- Is my child often unable to retell a story in order and in the appropriate sequence initially presented?
- Is my child showing difficulties following the social rules of conversation – for instance, appropriately 'taking turns' when conversing with another; standing at an appropriate distance from a listener, etc.?
- Is my child having difficulties memorising and using math facts at appropriate grade levels; for instance, memorising the 'times tables,' etc.?
- Is my child having difficulty understanding and applying grade-appropriate mathematical concepts and ideas?
- Does my child appear to be having difficulties knowing where to begin a task and then following through with the organisation and process of completing that task?
- Is my child having difficulty in class remaining focused and attentive at a developmentally appropriate level?

A teacher who observes a child over time in a classroom setting can provide parents with valuable information as to how the child is able to learn and function in school in all of the ways that he or she should be able to for his or her age and grade level. If teachers and parents feel that a child has apparent problems learning to read, write, listen, speak, or do math, then it is appropriate to further investigate those concerns. Such investigations may appropriately include a comprehensive evaluation by appropriate professionals – neuropsychologist, school psychologist, special education teacher, etc.– to clarify specific learning problems and also to rule out any other issues that may be affecting a student's educational progress and functioning.

Recommendations
- A single local commissioning service integrated with Health, Social Services, Housing and Education should be in place which will then show positive links between assessment and treatment between community specialist services, care management based on collaborative partnerships between primary and secondary care as well as with families and the person with ID from BME background. Power and control in the form of citizen and self-advocacy needs

to be in place so that the BME person with ID can have choices of where they live, how they live, how they maintain their ethnic, religious and cultural identity. Person-centred processes where a BME person will have control over these processes should be in place. This must include the importance of social model of disability, culturally competent and inclusive, be well prepared to be in control of the meeting and its processes, have communication passports (if necessary,) a health plan which may need psychological/therapeutic work plan in place (if necessary).

- For the helping profession to focus on social processes and institutional practices rather than the individualised focus on the client/person, that is for change to occur at personal and political levels and for the helping professional to become knowledgeable and familiar with the concepts of unconscious bias towards people from BME backgrounds, people with disabilities, people of different gender and sexuality.

- A single local commissioning service integrated with health and social services if necessary, needs to be in place.

- Training on an on-going rather than one-off basis needs to be provided to the helping professionals to understand their own values, their judgements and stereotypes belief that can affect the person with ID from BME background.

- Training in anti-oppressive practices and minimising the power differential within society works best with a model of empowerment for the BME person with ID and their carers. Anti-discriminatory and anti-oppressive training needs to be provided to practitioners at primary and secondary levels of care and treatment. GPs need to be more informed about mental health and other co-morbid problems for their clients with ID. Whereas community teams including psychologists, psychotherapists and counsellors work with their clients on the power differential, which exists within the structured organisation of the NHS, Social Care Services and the Education sector.

- Person-centred planning and development of care pathways needs to be established with the person's ethnic, cultural and spiritual needs being taken in to account, including hearing the voice of the person and their advocate or carers (as and when necessary).

- The ethnocentric knowledgebase of western therapy lacks acknowledgement of the detailed understanding of client's religious and spiritual beliefs which then influences the thinking about health, mental wellbeing, mental illness and treatment. The continual use of the ethno and Eurocentric perspective leads BME people with ID and their carer to mistrust services and the treatment offered due to the inherent fear of racism, discrimination, and stereotyped thinking of BME people with ID not being able to verbalise appropriately their emotional difficulties or to benefit from talking therapies and being subject to strong anti-psychotic medication and electro convulsive therapy.

- Consultation process and interviewing skills are key in terms of getting an accurate picture of the difficulties and or emotional problems experienced by the persons with ID from BME background. It would be important for the helping profession to develop appropriate sensitive practice using evidence-based therapy within different theoretical schools (analytical) cognitive behavioural, humanistic approaches that focuses exclusively on the client rather than the theory.

- Therapeutic training of psychologists and counsellors needs to focus on the client with ID and to focus more extensively on the relationship between the helping professional and the client, working with the here – and – now to facilitate holistic change for the person with ID.
- Helping professionals need to be offered training in mental health care to appreciate how culture, ethnicity, class and discrimination influences attitudes, expression of distress and help seeking behaviour on the part of the BME client with ID and his/her carer.
- There is a sense of duty and obligation that the helping professional acquires the knowledge and the ability and skills to meet the social and psychological needs of BME people with ID. Race equality, inclusivity and cultural capability training needs to be offered to the helping professional, which includes:
  - Having a deeper understanding of inequality, discrimination and disadvantage suffered by the person with ID and his/her position within Society.
  - Working with the person's loss of identity and self-esteem leading to over dependence on statutory services rather than appropriate community services as provided by the Black voluntary sector.
  - Learning about one's own prejudices, unconscious biases, stereotyped thinking and attitudes, and acknowledging them in understanding and working with 'the other'.
  - Exploring the issue that double discrimination is not the result of neutral objective intentions in the welfare system and in the helping profession but the result of selective experience and interests of institutions and organisations who attribute cultural stereotypes and generalisation about 'the other'.
  - Being preoccupied with the culture of the person with ID resulting in the helping professional basing all their thinking and therapeutic practice on cultural differences leading to a victim blaming approach.
  - Understanding the cultural bias that exists in the assessment procedures based on a white British standardisation norm which bears little relationship to the everyday life of the BME person with ID and his/her family. For example, assessment done to a person rather than with them or by them in assessing the person's abilities.
  - Adhering to ethical practice where the helping professional avoids harm and practices safely with a person with ID. The helping professional to think about ethical conflicts and dilemmas and to be aware of their own (westernised) values and beliefs of psychotherapy and counselling and its negative impact on people with ID as well as people with ID coming from BME backgrounds. They need to demonstrate their own ethical practice in terms of upholding professional standards of conduct, their professional role and obligation, respect for the autonomy of the client, maintenance of confidentiality and to be genuinely be emphatic to the 'other' (Nadirshaw, 2014).
  - Receiving appropriate supervision is a key task for the helping professional with the supervisor being trained and being competent in work with people with BME backgrounds as well as work with people with ID.

– The helping professional needs to work through the fears and assumptions about the 'other' – particularly when they have lost the fundamental acceptance of the person. The use of Reflective Practice and its importance should be encouraged as the helping professional may make decisions about their clients which may have profound impact on their lives – particularly as their personal and professional values influence a number of aspects of the therapeutic process and relationship (Milton, 2018).

Social factors of inequality, unemployment, disadvantage, racism and prejudice, poor housing and sexism might need to be brought into the therapeutic discourse with the client, with the helping professional being aware of its consequences on the client. For example, stigma and inequality, disadvantage and oppression for the person with ID coming from a BME background having to confront his or her shame, fear, isolation, loneliness and rejection and lack of choice within mainstream society and mainstream service.

Professor Zenobia Nadirshaw
Clinical Psychologist

References

Alan Mozes, Healthday Reporter (Nov, 2018). https://medicalxpress.com/news/2018-11-syn-drome-adults-death-dementia.html

Baxter, C., Poonia, K., Ward, L. & Nadirshaw, Z. (1990). *Double discrimination. Issues and Services for people with Learning Difficulties from Black and Ethnic Minority Communities.* Kings Fund Centre

Beail, N. (2016). *Psychological therapies and people who have intellectual disabilities.* BPS Division of Clinical Psychology and Royal College of Psychiatrists.

Costello H. & Bouras N. (2006) Assessment of mental health problems in people with ID (https://www.researchgate.net/profile/Helen_Costello/publication/6469245_Assessment_of_mental_health_problems_in_people_with_intellectual_disabilities/links/54be52f60cf218da9391e4a3.pdf)

Department of Health (2001). Valuing People: A new strategy for ID for the 21st Century (m 5086 HMSO London.

Emerson, E. & Hatton, C. (2007) – The Mental Health of Children and Adolescents with Learning Disability in Britain. Institute of Health Research. Lancaster University. https://www.lancaster.ac.uk/staff/emersone/FASSWeb/Emerson_07_FPLD_MentalHealth.pdf

Gates, B. & Wilberforce (2004). Chapter 1, "The nature of Learning disability". In B. Gates (Ed.) (2004) *Intellectual Disabilities. Towards Inclusion. 4th edn.* Churchill Livingstone – Elsevier Science.

Grant, M. (1985). Classification criteria, epidemiology and causation. In M. Grant, J. Bicknell & S. Hollins (Eds.) *Mental handicap: A multidisciplinary approach.* London: Balliere Tindall.

Hemings, C. (2018). Mental health in intellectual disabilities. A complete introduction to assessment, intervention, care & support. 5th edition. Brighton: Pavillion Publishing.

Hughes-McCormack, L.A., Rydzewska, E., Henderson, A. & MacIntyre, C. (2018). Prevalence of mental health conditions and relationship with general health in a whole-country population of people with ID compared with the general population – Volume 3, Issue 5. Online: https://doi.org/10.1192/bjpo.bp.117.005462

Jackson, T. & Beail, N. (2013). The practice of individual psychodynamic psychotherapy with people who have intellectual disabilities. Nigel Beail abstracts pages 108–123. Published online 6 June 2013.

Nadirshaw, Z. (2014). Making the invisible visible, the relationship when working with people with intellectual disabilities. In D. Charura & S. Paul *The therapeutic relationship handbook.* London: McGraw Hill.

Nadirshaw, Z. (1997). Cultural issues. In J. O'Hara and A. Sperlinger (Eds.) *Adults with ID. A practical approach for Health Professionals.* Chichester: Wiley.

Smiley, E. (2004). Epidemiology of mental health problems in adults with ID: An update. *Advances in Psychiatric Treatment, 11,* 214–222.

Taylor, J., Lyndsay, B. & Willner, P. (2008). *CBT for People with Intellectual Disabilities: Emerging Evidence, Cognitive Ability and IQ Effects – Volume 36, Special Issue 6 (Developments in the Theory and Practice of Cognitive and Behavioral Therapies* (Nov 2008).

The Royal College of Psychiatrists (2004). Psychotherapy and ID Council Report (CR116) Online: www.rcpsych.ac.uk/files/pdfversion/cr116.pdf

The Royal College of Psychiatrists (2011). Minority Ethnic Communities & Specialist Learning Disability Services. Report of the Faculty of Psychiatry of Learning Disability Working Group. London RC Psych.

Sinason, V. (1992). *Mental handicap and the human condition: New approaches from the Tavistock.* London: Free Association Books.

Vickers, A. (1994). *Intellectual disabilities, health options, complementary therapies for cerebral palsy and related conditions.* London: Element books Ltd.

Vickers, A. (1994) *Massage and aromatherapy. A guide for help professionals.* Cheltenham: Stanley Thornes Ltd.

Wolfensberger, W. & Glen, L. (1975). PASS 3. Programme analysis of service system – A method for the Qualative Evolution of human services. Toronto National Institute on Mental retardation, 3rd edition.

Wolfensberger, W. & Thomas, S. (1983). Programme analysis of service systems; implementation of Normalisation goals (PASSING) Toronto. National Institute of Mental Retardation.

Mentoring and ethnic minorities: A much missed opportunity within organisations

Roxane L. Gervais

The mentoring process is one that adds value to new employees, as well as more established employees, due to the support and developmental opportunities that it offers. It is a two-way relationship between a more experienced worker and one, either new to the workplace, or who wishes to change or advance her/his career options and opportunities. It has been proposed that mentoring should be seen as an essential part of the workplace, in terms of developing individuals and one of the factors that has a strong business case as regards to its implementation (Clutterbuck, 2014). However, while this may be relevant for some organisations, it may not be for others.

As with any process, there exists different understandings, interpretations and definitions of what it actually involves. In this scenario, one definition that I prefer and one I use when I mentor colleagues is 'A confidential one-to-one relationship in which an individual uses a more experienced person as a sounding board and for guidance. It is a protected, non-judgemental relationship, which facilitates a wide range of learning, experimentation and development. It is built on mutual regard, trust and respect.' (Business Wales, 2019). However, there are two other definitions that I think are relevant in this instance, as they specifically focus on the work context. They outline that it is 'A process in which one person (mentor) is responsible for overseeing the career and development of another person (mentee) outside the normal manager-subordinate relationship in an organisation.' (Collin, 1979; Nkomo et al., 2018, p.212), and is 'A protected relationship in which experimentation, exchange and learning can occur and skills, knowledge and insight be developed' (Mumford, 1993, p.103). The protected, developmental, as well as the knowledge and insight aspects of mentoring are essential within the work environment.

The mentor's role is diverse and includes opening doors (metaphorically) for the mentee; acting as a coach as well as a counsellor; advising the mentee; being a sounding board, as well as a guide; being a role model; a tutor; providing information, knowledge, and wisdom; providing managerial and or emotional support; and confronting problems, behaviours and relationships (Mumford, 1993). The mentor's role usually moves beyond the challenges within the workplace but can include discussions on issues that may happen at home. This is expected, as the work-life interface does not consist of two entities, but rather is one in which the boundaries of both blur and interact on each other. It is expected that the mentor will have a certain level of competencies and experience before agreeing to take on this type of relationship.

While there is no established context for what drives mentoring within organisations, it may be advantageous to consider which, from three different types of mentoring (UCDavis, 2018), an organisation may wish to use. This can focus on the traditional one-on-one form of mentoring in which the mentee and mentor are matched, either through a programme or pursuing a suitable individual on their own. In this mentoring relationship, the mentee-mentor partners agree on a structure and timeframe, which they design, or they can use one that has been established by a formal mentoring programme. The second style involves *distance mentoring*, which accommodates two parties (or a group) who are in different locations; it is known also as 'virtual' mentoring. The third relationship is group mentoring and consists of a single mentor, who is matched with a cohort of mentees. In this format, the mentor and mentees are provided with a programme structure, with the mentor directing the progress, pace and activities of the relationship.

The *traditional one-on-one form of mentoring* is the type of programme I use when mentoring. This seems to be the default for most situations and worked well for the programmes in which I was involved. I have mentored five individuals thus far, but only one was from a black and other minority ethnic (BME) group. The others were all white, mainly women, with one man. The literature has noted that the female mentor and male mentee is not the 'norm' in mentoring relationships (O'Neill & Blake-Beard, 2002). The male mentee asked me to be his mentor, while I was assigned the four women. My BME mentee was selected as part of a mentoring programme to develop ethnic minorities within the organisation. However, from the onset, the mentees were informed that promotions at the end of the programme was not a possibility. Despite this, it was a welcomed programme as many of the mentees had not been exposed to developmental opportunities previously, despite having extensive tenure with the organisation. Further, they worked mainly in administrative roles and were rarely encouraged to work outside that area. It is important to acknowledge that minority employees are less likely to get or to seek mentors, unless this occurs as part of a formal mentoring programme (Dobbin & Kalev, 2016), and this is different from white men who tend to find mentors without assistance. However, Thomas (1993) highlighted the importance of developmental relationships for both minority and white managers, which translated into higher salaries, bonuses, and overall compensation than for those mangers who did not have mentors (Roche, 1979). More interestingly, mentoring programmes increased the number of diverse managers in organisations; these on average consisted of a nine per cent up to 24 per cent increase of black, Hispanic, and Asian-American women, and Hispanic and Asian-American men in senior levels (Dobbin & Kalev, 2016).

The context of mentoring differs and can involve two broad types of mentoring, i.e. career and psychosocial functions (Kram, 1985). A career function allows the mentee to gain exposure and visibility, coaching, sponsorship, protection and challenging assignments. It is expected that these areas would support/advance the mentee's professional status in the organisation. The psychosocial function centres on role modelling, counselling, acceptance and confirmation, and friendship. These areas allow the mentees to enhance their competence, confidence, effectiveness and esteem. Both are important and the use of either would depend on those areas the mentee wished to develop.

Barriers to mentoring for minority groups

From the information detailed, it would seem that mentoring programmes within organisations would be valued and encouraged. However, Ragins and Cotton (1991) acknowledged that there are five barriers that may prevent new employees, and this will include young women specifically, but is not exclusive to this group, from wishing to have a mentoring relationship: the lack of access to potential mentors, the fear of rejection by the desired mentor when trying to initiate a mentoring relationship, the unwillingness of a desired mentor, the fear of disapproval of others in the immediate work environment, and the fear of sexual misconception when trying to initiate a mentoring relationship. The literature acknowledges that sexual misunderstanding, in terms of cross gender mentorships, i.e. male mentor and female mentee, is one of the reasons that many women have tended to have challenges in seeking and gaining male mentors at work (Noe, 1988; O'Neill & Blake-Beard, 2002). These barriers would be very relevant also for BME workers.

These barriers could be reduced at the organisational level. Kram (1985) observed that one of the key hurdles to establishing mentoring within organisations was due to an organisational reward system that did not support relationship building. She recommended that organisations could address this obstacle by promoting mentoring education, which in turn would create a learning-centred work environment. Some of the ways that this could occur was by acknowledging and perhaps rewarding those individuals who choose to mentor others, by ensuring that the organisation's work structure encourages teamwork and collaboration, and that leaders set the standard as the exemplars in the development of colleagues and junior workers (Kram, 1985; Kram & Hall, 1996). Dobbin and Kalev (2016) support the focus on more equity, specifically teamwork and collaboration, to improve relationships within organisations.

While the outcomes that mentoring brings are well-documented (e.g. Allen et al., 2004; Dashper, 2018), in terms of for example, career advancement, developmental opportunities, and building confidence to take on new challenges, there are disparities still in who profits the most from such programmes. As such, in determining who gains the most within the organisational context, the gendered organisation (Acker, 1990) has to be considered, as it is structured to support men's development and advancement, especially into leadership positons, rather than women's (Acker, 2009). This discussion is relevant also to mentoring relationships that are influenced by not only the gendered process within organisations, but as well by the wider societal systems and power dynamics that have been shaped by patriarchal laws, slavery, and homophobic secrecy (Fletcher & Ragins, 2007). In this context it can be reasoned that diverse groups and the support that they receive within organisations, will not be extensive in terms of the mentoring process. There is research that details the benefits for organisations when diversity is welcomed and is inherent in their structure. This will include being more likely to report a growth in market share or gain access to new markets (Hewlett & Wingfield, 2015), while more diverse boards tend to support a positive impact on firm value (Campbell & Mínguez-Vera, 2008). Despite this, Dashper (2018) asserts that women are the ones required to adjust to the business structure, i.e. the masculine norm, as well as to improve to allow their business performance to be accepted as equal to their male colleagues. Women may wish to use mentoring as part of their development. This rationale may extend to other groups, i.e. those identifying as BME.

Value to organisations of engaging BME groups in mentoring programmes

In today's workplaces, the concept of inclusivity and diversity is ever present. However, the challenge remains in gaining a fully inclusive and diverse organisations. As organisations respond to the bottom line, Hunt, Layton and Prince (2015) noted that diversity provides a competitive advantage. While, O'Neill (2002) indicated that if organisations want to effect change and remain competitive, they have to remove those barriers that keep women and ethnic minority groups from positions of power. One way to do this is to get them into mentoring relationships. Other researchers have supported that recommendation, e.g. Hunt, Layton and Prince (2015).

Kram and Ragins (2007) support the premise that the mentoring relationship is one that leads to and develops relational outcomes. This is manifested in the transferable skills and competencies between the two parties in terms of effective communication, which may include those skills relating to effective communication, empathic listening, personal learning, knowledge transfer, adaptability, emotional intelligence, self-reflection, self-awareness, and other indicators of personal growth. They posit further that these are competencies and behaviours that will transfer across other relationships, across time and in different settings, both in and outside the workplace. The outcomes from mentoring has the potential to impact on a wider range of relationships outside the initial duo; it may even result in the creation and sustenance of high-quality developmental networks.

Purpose

This chapter explores the value of mentoring to diverse groups within workplaces, especially those who consider themselves to be from BME groups. When exploring diversity within organisations, it is critical to consider intersectionality also. This is due to its importance in taking account of those intertwining interactions, i.e. gender, age, race, ethnicity, nationality and other categories of 'difference' among and between individuals, and the outcomes of these interactions in terms of power, especially when they facilitate the overlapping and interdependent systems of discrimination or disadvantage and inequality (Crenshaw, 1989; Davis, 2008). In order to determine the impact, a literature review was undertaken, and this will be supplemented by my personal experiences of acting as a mentor to a BME junior colleague.

Method

Due to the context of this chapter, it was necessary to determine the research that has been undertaken in terms of gauging the relevance of the topic to researchers and organisations. The PsychSource database (https://psychsource.bps.org.uk/view/index.html) was searched using six various terms. These included 'Mentor BME', which realised 142 journal articles, I reviewed the abstracts of these and downloaded 13 articles, of which I used six. The next term 'Mentor workplace diversity' realised 2288 results. I reviewed the first one hundred abstracts. This was due to the fact that some of the material from the first search, 'Mentor BME', were appearing in the second search. This search did not provide any material that focused on mentoring and diversity in the context of the work environment. Three further researches were undertaken using the phrases: 'Mentor workplace diversity inequality' ($N = 2726$, zero material was found); 'Mentor workplace diversity inequality black' ($N = 3346$', one article was found and reviewed); 'Mentor workplace diversity intersectional' ($N = 2466$), one article was found and reviewed; and 'Mentor workplace race' ($N = 1685$, zero material was found). These last four phrases, as with the second, continue to generate the same material identified previously.

An internet search provided slightly more relevant results. I used the following term 'mentoring diverse employees', which realised a further nine articles/chapters. I used seven of these. I reviewed a further six articles, gained from the references in the internet articles/chapters, and used five of these. Much of the material, including one that I sourced from PsychSource and one from the internet, was on mentoring diverse young people. These two did not add to an understanding of mentoring in the workplace.

This lack of research in respect of mentoring and race has been noted (Blake-Beard et al., 2007). O'Neill in 2002, stated that even though it is important to mentor women and ethnic minority groups, it was only in the 1990s that the focus of race and gender on mentoring started to gain more interest. In addition, there seems to be a finite number of persons who undertake research in this area, which may restrict what can be ascertained.

Due to the inadequacy of research on mentoring and race, I used research in respect of women, typically considered a 'minority' group in terms of career development, to assess what is feasible for BMEs in the workplace. In addition, most of the research is not recent.

An overview of the evidence

As outlined in the review of the method, there seems to exist limited research on mentoring among BME groups. There is material on how to implement diversity mentioning programmes (e.g. Clutterbuck, 2012; Ragins & Kram, 2007), but there is less information on the challenges faced by BME workers in getting support through a mentoring process. In 2007, Blake-Beard et al. recognised the lack of knowledge about the types of mentoring experiences that BME workers have in organisations. In this respect, the comment by Thomas in 1990 on the lack of research on work-centred developmental relationships in terms of the experiences of racial minorities continues to exist. Despite this, it is acknowledged that mentoring is one of the ways that organisations can retain diverse workers (Musser, 2001; Sadri & Tran, 2002). The limited information that is available makes it difficult to get a realistic understanding of the 'true' benefits that mentoring brings to BME workers. However, any developmental opportunity that can be provided to BME workers would allow them to perhaps gain confidence and choose to take on new or more challenging responsibilities. My BME mentee was very reserved at the start of the programme, and to some extent, still is, but she has taken on more responsibility and is more assured of who she is, in terms of her work role, than she was before the programme.

Power within organisations

The concept of power within organisations and its impact on the mentoring relationship is one of the reasons proposed for the challenges faced by minority (ethnic) groups within organisations. Power is viewed as a perceptually-based phenomenon, wherein perceptions of power are affected by gender and ethnic stereotypes; those in the minority within the organisation are less likely to have power, due to holding lower ranks (O'Neill & Blake-Beard, 2002; Ragins, 1997).

This acknowledgement of minority groups not having power within organisations resonates with one of my mentees. My BME mentee found it difficult to challenge some of the behaviours of her colleagues as she was in the minority, i.e. as the sole BME person, in her team. Of course, she found it difficult to discuss her colleagues' behaviours with others in the organisation as she felt it would not be given the gravitas that it deserved and in particular how these behaviours having increased her workload, would be addressed. We discussed various options for her to ensure she completed her tasks while ensuring a collegial environment, but to not take on unnecessarily the responsibilities of others in her team.

Power featured also in some of my other mentoring relationships. Some of these were not as successful as others. This may be due to Thomas's (1993) assertion that effective mentoring relationships would be difficult to achieve in some situations. These are when cross-racial mentoring, racial taboos, and the history of power relations between groups, along with those social identities that form those relational interactions that are essential to the mentoring connection between the mentor and the mentee, are underlying parts of the process. These may not necessarily be addressed between the parties and allow both persons to move forward. Further, the inherent power dynamics may not wish for a successful mentoring outcome when cross-racial mentoring occurs.

Establishing and developing relationships

One of the challenges faced by BME workers is that mentoring programmes have followed a model based on what would be suitable for the majority/white male archetypes, but this approach does not take into account the needs of the other groups who are present within organisations (Blake-Beard, Murrell, & Thomas, 2007). The research shows that in some organisations the mentoring programme is part of an inclusive network that supports the transfer of power between men (Simon, 2019). There are challenges when diverse individuals try to find a senior colleague who is willing to act as their mentor and work to maintain this relationship. O'Neill (2002) suggests that this may be due to gender and racial prejudice and discrimination that occur within organisations. There is evidence to show the inequalities between white male and non-white female in terms of establishing mentoring relationships within organisations, which in turn led to compensation differences (Dreher & Cox, 1996).

In terms of some of the other challenges for women in obtaining a mentor (Ragins & Cotton, 1991), one of these is due to women having fewer formal and informal opportunities from which to build relationships within the workplace that could lead to mentoring or other support. Even when women have mentors, they are less likely than men to benefit from this relationship, in terms of promotions or other ways to enhance their careers (Dashper, 2018). These findings could transfer to issues that BME groups encounter when attempting to gain a mentor. There is research that illustrate positive outcomes, such as showing that gender bias in respect of mentoring did not exist in specific organisations (Arnold & Johnson, 1997). Another study found that women did not observe that their gender was a barrier to getting engaged in mentoring relationships (Blickle et al., 2010).

Blake-Beard et al. (2007) have highlighted the paucity of research in terms of the negative impact of mentoring due to race. The mentoring relationship that I had with a BME colleague was positive for both of us and we are still in contact. It was the same for the male mentee. It was not that the other mentoring relationships were negative, but the relational aspects of the connections may not have developed to a stage in which the cross-race issue was not a factor.

Any relationship has to be nurtured if it is to become one in which both parties feel comfortable, this is especially when the physical attributes between the mentor and mentee may differ. In this respect, a very process driven approach to the mentoring relationship may not work for BME groups.

Acknowledging differences

The barriers that women face is even more relevant when they are compared with individuals from other diverse backgrounds, such as race and ethnicity. This can include receiving less task-related, social-related, and career-related support from mentors whose nationality differ from their mentees (Feldman et al., 1999). This would lead to limited opportunities to advance the mentees' careers or enhance their learning and development.

Thomas (1993) in his study on cross-race relationships found that the pairs used two strategies to address their racial differences. This was either through denying and suppressing it or by discussing it openly. When both parties in the mentor relationship favoured the same strategy, then this led to a more supportive mentor-mentee relationship. However, Blake-Beard, Murell and Thomas (2007) acknowledged that race has to be seen as relevant in cross-race mentoring relationships. They note that when it is not recognised that the unique complexities, issues, and insights that occur in cross-race relationships, would also not be acknowledged and addressed. This may affect adversely such relationships and they advocated for race becoming more visible in organisations and as well in mentoring relationships; this will support the acceptance of race as a part of organisational life.

One proposed way to be more inclusive in the mentoring process is for organisations to engage in diversity mentoring (Clutterbuck, 2012). While this seems a useful process, it is one that highlights still the physical differences, in terms of race, ethnicity etc., between individuals in organisations. The focus of mentoring should be on the individual, rather than letting individual difference be a relevant criterion in the relationship. If the mentoring process is to be more inclusive, then the persons in the relationship should be viewed as mentor/mentee. As in any relationship, the differences and similarities, regardless of race and ethnicity, will emerge as the relationship develops.

The relevance of mentoring to mental and emotional health

In 1990, Thomas found that black individuals were able to source developmental relationships within organisations, but these were more likely to be gained across departments outside of their own. Moreover, the mentees gained more psychosocial support when they were in same-race relationships. Holder, Jackson and Ponterotto's research (2015) found that black women with sponsors and mentors at their workplace felt empowered, as well as accepted that their presence was validated in the workplace. Holder et al.'s research indicated as well that this support system assisted them in coping better with the microaggressions that they experienced at work. The support provided by mentoring may work to reduce job stress experienced by professional women, and who frequently do not have a peer group within the organisation to rely on for psychological support (Nelson & Quick, 1985).

This is relevant to Kram's (1985) two types of mentoring approach: career and psychosocial. It may be more useful at times for BMEs to receive the psychosocial aspect of mentoring, before the career function. These may be done in conjunction, but it depends on the mentee and his/her needs.

Overall, despite the mixed findings, it is evident that the inequality in terms of development opportunities that are available to BME workers, continues to exist. Despite the limited organisational research about the positive or negative impact of mentoring for BME groups, it is relevant still to state that the lack of mentoring of BME workers may be a missed opportunity for organisations. They may not be getting the full performance levels of workers, who may have the potential, but may not have the support to take on new challenges and prospects. The chapter ends with recommendations that may encourage organisations to provide this support through mentoring programmes.

Moving forward
Supporting change at the organisational level

Leenders, Bleijenbergh and Van den Brink's research (2019) found that a continuous transformational change programme, with interventions at the individual level, e.g. creating safe spaces to have open conversations about individuals' experiences, as well as at the structural (organisational) level, e.g. identifying and experimenting with new work practices, assisted in reducing the norms and practices that occur in gendered organisations. This could apply also to how diverse workers, outside of the gender dynamic, are treated within organisations. They found that five actions were more likely to contribute to transformational change. These were: cross-mentoring, questioning what is taken for granted, repeating participation and individual stories, facilitating peer support networks and addressing and equipping all participants as change agents. This approach may assist BME groups, especially in the mentees taking on the mantle of mentors. Busch (1985) established that those who are mentored, then go on to mentor others. This could be one way to promote mentoring among BME groups and provide developmental opportunities within these groups.

Get more BME workers to be mentors and mentees

It is important to get more individuals from BME backgrounds involved in the mentoring process as both mentors and mentees. It would be accepted that mentees would benefit, but there is increasing evidence that mentors gain significant outcomes from being part of that process (e.g. Ghosh & Reio, 2013).

Create an organisational climate that is conducive to mentoring and learning

As Hunt et al. (2015) have highlighted, diversity matters. Further, as researchers have advocated, e.g. Hunt et al. (2015), Kossek, Lobel and Brown (2006), the implementation of formal and informal mentoring programmes is one of the ways to promote an inclusive work environment. This is especially to provide mentoring for BME groups. As noted above, Kram (1985) recommended the implementation of an organisational reward system that supports relationship building. This is even more important when BME workers are involved, as they may struggle to emerge from the roles they occupy within the organisation, as well as the lack of competencies that they may not be perceived to possess.

Ensure that mentors have the required competencies

It is imperative that the number of mentors available to work with mentees increases. Despite this need, it is essential that any mentor has the required competencies to support her or his mentee to allow the individual to develop and achieve.

Respect individual differences

As this chapter has outlined, there are societal, power structures, stereotypes and historical relationships that influence how organisations have been structured and which continue to be part of how organisations function. These in turn drive how individuals interact in the workplace. While legislation has helped with these perceptions and behaviours, in order to ensure that workers are developed, when using mentoring as a development tool, it is essential that all individual differences are respected. As Kram and colleagues (Kram, 1985; Kram & Hall, 1996) have proposed, standards and behaviours have to be promoted from the top, meaning that senior leaders should lead by example and mentor BME workers.

Explore cross-mentoring programmes

Cross-mentoring, is a process in which individuals are paired according to their skill sets, as much as their diversity. It is one way that could help to reduce the stereotypes that exist about BME groups in organisations. This type of relationship allows individuals to display their business strengths and competencies and support each other on projects in order to develop better as an individual or as part of a team.

Dr Roxane L. Gervais
Occupational Psychologist

References

Acker, J. (1990). Hierarchies, occupations, bodies: A theory of gendered organizations. *Gender and Society, 4*(2), 139–158. https://doi.org/10.1177/089124390004002002

Acker, J. (2009). From glass ceiling to inequality regimes. *Sociologie du Travail, 51*(3), 199–217. doi:10.1016/j.soctra.2009.03.004

Allen, T.D., Eby, L.T., Poteet, M.L., Lentz, E. & Lima, L. (2004). Career benefits associated with mentoring for protégés: A meta-analysis. *Journal of Applied Psychology, 89*(1), 127–136. http://dx.doi.org/10.1037/0021-9010.89.1.127

Arnold, J. & Johnson, K. (1997). Mentoring in early career. *Human Resource Management Journal, 7*(4), 61–70. doi:10.1111/j.1748-8583.1997.tb00289.x

Blake-Beard, S.D., Murrell, A. & Thomas, D. (2007). Unfinished business: The impact of race on understanding mentoring relationships. In B.R. Ragins & K.E. Kram (Eds.) *The handbook of mentoring at work: Theory, research, and practice* (pp.223–248). Thousand Oaks, California: Sage Publications, Inc. http://dx.doi.org/10.4135/9781412976619.n9

Blickle, G., Schneider, P.B., Meurs, J.A. & Perrewé, P.L. (2010). Antecedents and consequences of perceived barriers to obtaining mentoring: A longitudinal investigation. *Journal of Applied Social Psychology, 40*(8), 1897–1920. doi:10.1111/j.1559-1816.2010.00644.x

Busch, J.W. (1985). Mentoring in graduate schools of education: Mentors' perceptions. *American Educational Research Journal, 22*(2), 257–265. https://doi.org/10.3102/00028312022002257

Business Wales. (2019). About Us. What is Business Wales Mentoring? Welsh Government. Retrieved from https://businesswales.gov.wales/mentoring/about-us

Campbell, K. & Mínguez-Vera, A. (2008). Gender diversity in the boardroom and firm financial performance. *Journal of Business Ethics, 83*(3), 435–451. doi:10.1007/s10551-007-9630-y

Clutterbuck, D. (2014). Everyone needs a mentor: Fostering talent at work (5th edn). London: Chartered Institute of Personnel and Development.

Clutterbuck, D. (2012). Understanding diversity mentoring. In D. Clutterbuck, K.M. Poulsen & F. Kochan (Eds.). Developing successful diversity mentoring programmes: An international casebook (pp.1–17). Maidenhead, Berkshire: McGraw Hill Education (UK).

Collin, A. (1979). Notes on some typologies of managerial development and the role of the mentor in the process of adaptation of the individual to the organisation. *Personnel Review, 8*(1), 10–14. https://doi.org/10.1108/eb055392

Crenshaw, K. (1989). Demarginalizing the intersection of race and sex: A black feminist critique of antidiscrimination doctrine, feminist theory and antiracist politics. *University of Chicago Legal Forum*, 1989(1), Article 8. Retrieved from http://chicagounbound.uchicago.edu/uclf/vol1989/iss1/8

Dashper, K. (2018). Challenging the gendered rhetoric of success? The limitations of women-only mentoring for tackling gender inequality in the workplace. *Gender, Work & Organisation, 26*(4), 541–557. doi:10.1111/gwao.12262

Davis, K. (2008). Intersectionality as buzzword: A sociology of science perspective on what makes a feminist theory successful. *Feminist Theory, 9*(1), 67–85. doi:10.1177/1464700108086364

Dobbin, F. & Kalev, A. (2016). Why diversity programs fail. *Harvard Business Review, July-August, 94*(7), 52–60. Retrieved from https://hbr.org/2016/07/why-diversity-programs-fail

Dreher, G.F. & Cox, T.H., Jr. (1996). Race, gender, and opportunity: A study of compensation attainment and the establishment of mentoring relationships. *Journal of Applied Psychology, 81*(3), 297–308. http://dx.doi.org/10.1037/0021-9010.81.3.297

Feldman, D.C., Folks, W.R. & Turnley, W.H. (1999). Mentor-protege diversity and its impact on international internship experiences. *Journal of Organizational Behavior, 20*(5), 597–611. doi:10.1002/(SICI)1099-1379(199909)20:5<597::AID-JOB977>3.0.CO;2-#

Fletcher, J.K. & Ragins, B.R. (2007). Stone Center Relational Cultural Theory: A window on relational mentoring. In B.R. Ragins & K.E. Kram (Eds.) *The handbook of mentoring at work: Theory, research, and practice* (pp.373–400). Thousand Oaks, California: Sage Publications, Inc. http://dx.doi.org/10.4135/9781412976619.n15

Ghosh, R. & Reio, T.G. (2013). Career benefits associated with mentoring for mentors: A meta-analysis. *Journal of Vocational Behavior, 83*(1), 106–116. doi:10.1016/j.jvb.2013.03.011

Hewlett, S.A. & Wingfield, T. (2015, June 11). Qualified Black women are being held back from management. Harvard Business Review. Retrieved from https://hbr.org/2015/06/qualified-black-women-are-being-held-back-from-management?referral=03758&cm_vc=rr_item_page.top_right

Holder, A.M.B., Jackson, M.A. & Ponterotto, J.G. (2015). Racial microaggression experiences and coping strategies of Black women in corporate leadership. *Qualitative Psychology, 2*(2), 164–180. http://dx.doi.org/10.1037/qup0000024

Hunt, V., Layton, D. & Prince, S. (2015). Diversity Matters. McKinsey & Company. Retrieved from https://www.mckinsey.com/~/media/mckinsey/business functions/organization/our insights/why diversity matters/diversity matters.ashx

Kossek, E.E., Lobel, S.A. & Brown, J. (2006). Human resource strategies to manage workforce diversity: Examining 'the business case'. In A.M. Konrad, P. Prasad & J.K. Pringle (Eds.) Handbook of workplace diversity (pp.53–74). London: SAGE Publications Ltd. doi:10.4135/9781848608092.n3

Kram, K.E. (1985). *Mentoring at work: Developmental relationships in organizational life.* Glenview, IL: Scott, Foresman.

Kram, K.E. & Hall, D.T. 1996. Mentoring in a context of diversity and turbulence. In E.E. Kossek & S.A. Lobel (Eds.) *Managing diversity: Human resource strategies for transforming the workplace* (pp.108–136). Cambridge, MA: Blackwell Business.

Kram, K.E. & Ragins, B.R. (2007).The landscape of mentoring in the 21st Century. In B.R. Ragins & K.E. Kram (Eds.) *The handbook of mentoring at work: Theory, research, and practice* (pp.659–692). Thousand Oaks, California: Sage Publications, Inc. http://dx.doi.org/10.4135/9781412976619.n27

Leenders, J., Bleijenbergh, I.L. & Van den Brink, M.C.L. (2019). Myriad potential for mentoring: Understanding the process of transformational change through a gender equality intervention. *Gender, Work & Organisation,* 1–16. doi:10.1111/gwao.12385

Mumford, A. (1993). *How managers can develop managers.* Aldershot, Hampshire: Gower.

Musser, L.R. (2001). Effective retention strategies for diverse employees. *Journal of Library Administration, 33*(1-2), 63–72. doi:10.1300/J111v33n01_06

Nelson, D.L. & Quick, J.C. (1985). Professional women: Are distress and disease inevitable? *Academy of Management Review, 10*(2), 206–218. http://dx.doi.org/10.2307/257963

Nkomo M.W., Thwala, W.D. & Aigbavboa, C.O. (2018). Human resource management and effects of mentoring on retention of employees in the construction sector: A literature review. In T. Andre (Ed.) Advances in Human Factors in Training, Education, and Learning Sciences (pp. 207–217). AHFE 2017. *Advances in Intelligent Systems and Computing, vol 596.* Springer, Cham. doi: https://doi.org/10.1007/978-3-319-60018-5_21

Noe, R. (1988). Women and mentoring: A review and research agenda. *Academy of Management Review, 13*(1), 65–78. doi:10.2307/258355

O'Neill, R.M. (2002). Gender and race in mentoring relationships: a review of the literature In D. Clutterbuck & B.R. Ragins (Eds.) Mentoring and diversity: An international perspective (pp.1–22). London: Routledge. Oxford: Butterworth-Heinemann.

O'Neill, R.M. & Blake-Beard, S.D. (2002). Gender barriers to the female mentor - male protégé relationship. *Journal of Business Ethics, 37*(1), 51–63. https://doi.org/10.1023/A:1014778017993

Ragins, B.R. (1997). Diversified mentoring relationships in organizations: A power perspective. *Academy of Management Review, 22*(2), 482–581. doi:10.2307/259331

Ragins, B.R. & Cotton, J.L. (1991). Easier said than done: Gender differences in perceived barriers to gaining a mentor. *The Academy of Management Journal, 34*(4), 939–951. doi:10.2307/256398

Ragins, B.R. & Kram, K.E. (Eds.) (2007). *The handbook of mentoring at work: Theory, research, and practice* (pp.373–400). Thousand Oaks, California: Sage Publications, Inc.

Roche, G.R. (1979). Much ado about mentors. *Harvard Business Review, 77*(1), 14–28.

Sadri, G. & Tran, H. (2002). Managing your diverse workforce through improved communication. *Journal of Management Development, 21*(3), 227–237. https://doi.org/10.1108/02621710210420291

Simon, S.J. (2019). Hollywood power brokers: Gender and racial inequality in talent agencies. *Gender, Work & Organisation, 1–17.* doi:10.1111/gwao.12365

Thomas, D.A. (1990). The impact of race on managers' experiences of developmental relationships (mentoring and sponsorship): An intra-organizational study. *Journal of Organizational Behavior, 11*(6), 479–492. doi:10.1002/job.4030110608

Thomas, D.A. (1993). Racial dynamics in cross-race developmental relationships. *Administrative Science Quarterly, 38*(2), 169–194. http://dx.doi.org/10.2307/2393410

UCDavis (2018). Types of Mentoring. The Regents of the University of California, Davis campus. Retrieved from https://hr.ucdavis.edu/departments/learning-dev/toolkits/mentoring/types

Therapist use of self to manage difference with minority ethnic clients

Lorraine Gordon

This chapter seeks to present some of the issues in transcultural therapy, it will consider how the literature may be applied to clinical practice. Firstly, this chapter locates culturally sensitive therapy within a contextual frame of reference. It affords an opportunity for the therapist to consider how the cultural difference between therapist and client, if any, may influence the therapeutic relationship whilst examining the issues of power and racism. The final section aims to provide therapists with insight into developing culturally sensitive practice skills. Based on case material from the author's own practice, it highlights the process of transcultural therapy. It offers an example of how therapists could include a consideration of cultural difference in therapy when assessing, formulating, hypothesising and selecting interventions. It also suggests how therapists might manage practice dilemmas.

Introduction

Being a Black counselling psychologist living and working in Britain means that a great deal of the author's clinical work has been with culturally distant clients namely, working with people who are from differing cultural and or ethnic backgrounds to one's own. Mainly through reflective practice, the author has come to appreciate that a therapist's perception of cultural diversity affects the validity and efficacy of one's approach. Thus, as a therapist this experience suggests that it is essential to be aware of how both the client's and one's own cultural identity impacts on the process of therapy. Developing culturally sensitive practice should be an integral part of continuous professional development in counselling psychology.

In this section, the context of transcultural therapy is established historically. In order to consider what culturally sensitive therapy is, it is necessary to place it within a historical perspective. The tale begins with migration to Britain in the 16th century. According to Lago and Thompson (1996), it is likely that West Africans first entered London in 1554. This is thought to have come about as a result of the growing trade between Britain and West Africa. At this time, some West Africans were sold to white households as servants. During the mid-eighteenth century, Britain became one of the leading slave-trading nations in the world. More recently, in the nineteenth century, the predominant migrant population to England has emanated from Ireland, Europe and the British Commonwealth (for example, the Caribbean: Lago & Thompson, 1996). The slave trade ended centuries ago. Unfortunately, however, some of the prejudice which was characteristic of those times remains (Beck, 2016). Kareem and Littlewood (1992) argue that British-born children whose parents migrated to Britain suffer the effects of 'culture shock' – a psychological reaction to living in a country where they are regarded as 'immigrants'. Lago and Thompson (1996) cite evidence that 4 out of 5 Afro-Caribbeans and 56 per cent of Asians described Britain as 'very' or 'fairly' racist. Notwithstanding the impact of colonialism where countries were often brutally invaded and ravished of their resources (Fernando, 2010).

The use of psychological approaches to therapy across cultures has been established for many years (Eleftheriadou, 1994). Therapist competence in attending to cultural processes is considered an essential component for effective treatment (Goodwin et al., 2018). Within the concept of transcultural therapy, the term 'trans' refers to the, 'active and reciprocal process involved' in working, 'across, through and beyond' cultural differences (D'Ardenne and Mahtani, 1989). The transcultural practitioner recognises the struggles clients from ethnic minorities may have had to face as a result of their ethnicity and begins to acknowledge this in therapy. Here, transcultural therapy is defined as a perspective on therapy where the therapist is aware of how both his/her own and the client's racial identity impact on the process of therapy and is sensitive in responding to the client's experience of ethnicity. Actively thinking about issues and practice of culturally sensitive therapy might prevent therapists recreating discriminatory processes within the context of therapy. Work on unconscious bias tells us it is possible to counteract organisational discrimination (Chao & Willaby, 2007). It could equip the therapist to be sensitive to what clients may have faced at societal and service levels. It may assist the therapist in working across, through and beyond cultural differences. This first section considered migration, slavery and present-day racism as the historical context within which culturally sensitive therapy in Britain is located.

Considering the therapist

Counselling psychologists will often encounter challenges whilst working transculturally. These challenges are related to the therapist's skill and knowledge base as well as to personal issues. They are linked to his/her awareness of how the same may be utilised across cultures. Here, the notion of 'universality' is taken to entail two related points. Firstly, it refers to the assumption that professionals should be able to work through, across and beyond all cultures (Kareem & Littlewood, 1992). Secondly, 'universality' includes the wider consideration that there is some identifiable presentation of mental illness across cultures. Further, that there exists a clear world-wide concept of mental health. However, it is postulated here that rather than being agreed cross-culturally, perceptions of what is 'normal' and what is 'abnormal' are largely informed by an individual's culture or subculture. Hence, notions of normality and abnormality are, to some extent, culture-specific and not universal to all groups (Eleftheriadou, 1994). Therefore, applying so-called 'universal' approaches will benefit the majority for whom they have been developed and further pathologise people from minority ethnic groups.

In their review, Cabral and Smith (2011) demonstrated patients had a moderately strong preference for a therapist from their own race/ethnicity. Kareem and Littlewood (1992) argue that for the professional, there are obvious challenges in attempting to work therapeutically with the culturally different. For example, a client from an Arab culture may respond to bereavement very differently to the way in which a therapist with experience solely from a Western culture would expect. Without knowledge of this cultural context, a therapist could find him/herself working on the assumption that the client's presentation is somehow pathological. However, a therapist from an Arab culture may consider the client's presentation to be within the accepted/normal range of responses. Lago and Thompson (1996) argue that in order to be in a position to respond therapeutically to the experience and views of people from ethnic minorities, therapists must acknowledge their cultural identity and the impact this may have on the therapeutic relationship. Further, Drinane, Owen, and Tao (2018) maintain that cultural discussions are essential to the process of psychological therapy and impact patient outcomes. They assert that clients who engage with their therapists openly experience more positive change through treatment than clients who conceal their culture (Drinane et al, 2018). Accordingly, it is important that therapists create environments that are welcoming of clients' cultural identities, perspectives, and worldviews. Reassuringly, perhaps, Kareem and Littlewood (1992) assert that it is possible for a client and therapist of differing ethnicity to engage in a therapeutic relationship. They maintain that this, 'involves the therapist being able to gather information' about the client's ethnicity and culture. It is considered here, that the challenge for the culturally distant therapist is to begin to *hear* the client and locate his/her experience within a socio-cultural/political context.

The present chapter now turns to the processes thought to be involved in the development of racial identity. Here, 'racial identity' is defined as a psychological construct about the self – associated with a personal perception of one's race, culture and ethnicity, which develops in relation to changing internal and external factors. Within transcultural therapy, the therapist first needs to perceive him/ herself as a racial being, then to assess where he/she is in terms of his/her own personal journey of racial identity. From here, the therapist can begin to consider where the client is in terms of the client's racial identity development. In the therapeutic relationship, each party's level of racial identity development is important (Carter, 1995). Fernando, (2010) discusses how the term 'identity' itself is based on 'ethnocentric assumptions' of individuality in Western psychology.

> *'Every worker in the mental health field should be trained to recognise the ways in which their own cultural upbringing is likely to have affected their perceptions of the problems which their clients bring ...'* (Murphy, 1986: in Lago & Thompson, 1996: p.14).

The above quote from Murphy (1986) cited in Lago and Thompson (1996) emphasises the impact the racial identity of a therapist can have on how clients' presenting problems are heard and valued. Thinking about issues related to racial identity within the process of forming a collaborative therapeutic relationship is paramount. It is suggested here that it is crucial for a therapist to have a sensitivity to the ramifications of the phase of both his/her own and the client's racial identity development in order to negotiate goals of therapy with the client. Therapists must be aware of their culturally informed beliefs, values, stereotypes and preconceived notions. Goals one would set with a client socialised within a Western culture may not be culturally congruent for a client from another culture. For example, it may be inappropriate to work towards the goal of enhancing the level of assertiveness with a female client who strongly identifies with an Indian culture.

There continues to be debate regarding the applicability of Western therapeutic approaches to ethnic groups. Wing, Sue and Sue (1999) argue that attrition rates among ethnic minorities in therapy settings are often related to the therapist's inability to correctly identify the stage of racial identity which their clients have achieved.

In summary, this section has considered the particular challenges the therapist might face in applying his/her skills and knowledge base to a culturally diverse population. It also examined the concept of universality in terms of the cultural specificity of the constructs of normality and abnormality. In this section, it was suggested that it is essential for the therapist to be aware of his/her own phase of racial identity development. Also, to have an awareness of where a client is in terms of the development of his/her racial identity. In the next section, the therapist is invited to consider how difference in culture based on race/ethnicity between a client and him/herself might affect the therapeutic relationship.

Managing difference in therapy

Having considered the therapist and examined the notion of racial identity, the focus in the present section is on managing difference in therapy. This part affords an opportunity for the therapist to consider how difference in culture within the therapeutic relationship may influence the relationship. Hence, this section aims to illuminate the issues of power and racism.

In terms of managing difference in therapy, the therapist should be aware of how power is perceived within the therapeutic relationship. Jones (1993) argues that the therapist is in a more powerful position than the client from the start of the relationship. She states that the therapist is on 'home territory' whether seeing the client within an organisational setting or the client's own home. This is so, as the therapist is in a familiar professional situation whereas the client may be unaccustomed to the roles taken in therapy (Jones, 1993).

Pinderhughes (1990) asserts that for the therapist, possessing an understanding of power dynamics in the relationship is a critical factor in the therapeutic process. Neglecting to analyse power relations may result in a therapist being more likely to engage in an oppressive relationship with a client (Jones, 1993). Further, D'Ardenne and Mahtani (1989) argue that the therapeutic alliance will not progress if the issue of power is not addressed. In a relationship which involves working across cultures, power dynamics can be more pronounced than they typically might be in therapy with a culturally close (Furnham & Bochner, 1986) client (Lago & Thompson, 1996). We all have our own prejudices and expectations. When a culturally distant (Furnham & Bochner, 1986) client and therapist are brought together within the context of a therapeutic relationship, one or the other may experience racism.

Although racism has been mentioned earlier in other sections of this chapter, here is the juncture at which a definition of the concept will be posed. This is the case as, in this discussion about transcultural therapy, racism within the therapeutic relationship is taken to be the height of cultural difference between therapist and client. Racism has been defined as, 'a prejudice against race... an activity within history and culture...where races are oppressed' (Kovel, 1984 cited in Carter, 1995: p.17). Another consideration which the author finds useful to include in a definition of racism is that it is 'prejudice plus power' (Lago & Thompson, 1996; Beck, 2016). This latter statement alludes to a critical factor in the concept of racism whereby the dominant culture possesses political and economic power within which prejudice is manifested. In addition, Wing Sue and Sue (1999) draw attention to the concept of 'unintentional racism'. They maintain that a well-intentioned majority ethnic group therapist may exude a covert form of bias of which he/she is unaware. They caution that this covert bias may have a phenomenal impact on the process of therapy. Here, the suggestion is that within the therapeutic relationship, racism may at times be subtle. Nonetheless, it is an example of how the effects of a power imbalance in the relationship might be born out.

Lago and Thompson (1996) maintain that in a therapeutic relationship with a client from a minority ethnic group, the white therapist has the power. Therefore, it is argued that in order to arrest the perpetuation of the construct of 'white superiority', the white therapist must be culturally sensitive (Lago & Thompson, 1996; Wing Sue & Sue, 1999). The suggestion is that therapists must be in a position to critically evaluate their own attitudes and expectations (D'Ardenne & Mahtani, 1989). This is particularly so as people who present to therapy typically consider that they need some form of help. Clients may be acutely aware of the power imbalance in the relationship. In many cases, immediately, the client offers him/herself as less 'psychologically competent/aware' and less powerful than the therapist. According to D'Ardenne and Mahtani (1989), the prevailing notion is that through being culturally sensitive, the transcultural therapist may begin to assist in redressing the power imbalance in the relationship. Acknowledging and tackling the notion of white superiority within therapy may facilitate this process. One suggestion is then, that in order to manage the difference that a power imbalance and racism in the therapeutic relationship affords, therapists should find an appropriate time during the assessment to discuss the issue of prejudice (D'Ardenne & Mahtani, 1989).

This chapter suggests that therapists should be wary of viewing the client's ethnicity as 'the problem' (D'Ardenne & Mahtani, 1989). Although it is important to consider culture, the therapist must also remember to consider individual differences. Further, the transcultural therapist should not aim to be 'colour-blind' which involves seeing black people as, 'white with black skin' (D'Ardenne & Mahtani, 1989; Wing Sue & Sue, 1999). D'Ardenne and Mahtani (1989) argue that being colour-blind is potentially harmful as it minimises the experience of the client from a minority ethnic group. How a therapist might manage difference when she/he is from a minority ethnic group and the client from the majority culture is discussed. The position of the minority ethnic person as, 'expert' goes against convention (Lago & Thompson, 1996). Although within the therapeutic relationship the therapist has power, a therapist from a minority ethnic group might find that some of his/her majority-culture clients communicate racist attitudes towards him/her (D'Ardenne & Mahtani, 1989). As therapists, it is important to note that by virtue of the nature of the relationship, the client is likely to be in a more vulnerable position than one's self. Where a therapist feels unsafe or unable to contain the process of therapy, addressing racism where appropriate, such issues should be taken to supervision so that the processes involved can be carefully examined (Schen & Greenlee, 2018).

In summary, this section aimed to provide an opportunity for the therapist to consider how a difference in culture between a client and him/herself might influence the therapeutic relationship. In order to do this, it discussed the issues of power and racism. The suggestion was made that there is a power imbalance within all therapeutic relationships linked with perceptions related to social construction. In order to form a useful therapeutic alliance, one of the necessary conditions is that a therapist who works with culturally distant clients should have an awareness of how to manage both his/her own and the client's racism. The section which follows uses some ideas which are based on case material from the author's own practice specifically to illuminate the process of transcultural therapy.

Culturally sensitive practice skills

Culturally adapted psychotherapies have been shown to be effective and favoured by patients and carers (Fung & Lo, 2017; Bhui et al., 2015). In the above section, factors affecting the therapeutic relationship were expounded in terms of managing difference in therapy. This section aims to provide therapists with insight into developing culturally sensitive practice skills. Based on case material from the author's own practice, it highlights the process of culturally sensitive therapy, and considers the impact of religion on the therapeutic process. It also provides an example of how therapists could include a consideration of cultural difference in therapy when assessing, formulating, hypothesising and selecting interventions. In addition, it indicates how therapists might manage practice dilemmas. It is hoped that what becomes clear through the presentation of the following case material is some of the challenges the author faced as a therapist working transculturally and how these were dealt with.

The 'Mohammed' family background information

This consideration of the process of transcultural therapy is based on the author's systemic work with a Turkish family who embrace Islam. The author was aware (through the previous attempts of my colleagues), that asking members of the family to meet for sessions at the team base might prove fruitless. The family were given the choice of appointments either at the team base or at their home. 'Aisha' (wife, mother and grandmother in Figure 1) telephoned the base to suggest home visits; the family were seen in the living room of their home. The author was aware this might render one susceptible to the 'games' they play – affecting the chances that one might become embroiled in the rules of the family (Jones, 1993). However, the author prepared to visit them knowing that there would be time and space to scrutinise these issues in supervision.

The identified client was a 21-year-old female, the youngest of two sisters. She has been referred to as 'Aida', to preserve her anonymity Aida and her family were seen within the context of an NHS mental health community team. Aida lives with her father Mustafa and her mother Aisha. Mustafa is an engineer and Aisha works in the home. Aida's sister Candan is 24-years-old. She is married with two children (see Figure 1 Genogram).

Leading up to the referral, Aida's involvement with the mental health team had been characterised by poor engagement in activities over a 15-month period. Following these difficulties within the team, the author received a referral from Aida's nurse. It requested a psychological assessment of Aida's 'independence', in view of her mental health needs. Aida had been involved in a road traffic accident (RTA) when she was four years old. In light of her previous accident, on her first psychiatric admission, Aida was referred for an EEG and a CT scan. Neither of these investigations pointed to any abnormalities following the RTA. She had a five-year history of bipolar affective disorder. Her paternal grandmother had a diagnosis of schizophrenia and her mother was diagnosed as clinically depressed.

Assessing

During the initial assessment phase, taking a transcultural perspective to therapy which enabled me to begin to get a sense of how important and influential their Muslim faith was in their daily lives. Engaging in this process was designed to begin to establish my credentials as a culturally sensitive practitioner (D'Ardenne & Mahtani, 1989). It was essential to assess their view on the problems they were facing within a sociocultural/political context (Lago & Thompson, 1996). This included discussion about what they felt had triggered the problem and a consideration of the methods that had already been used to address it. Also, this was the place for me to begin to be curious about how the problems they had identified fit or did not fit with their perception of health and illness within both Turkish and Western societies. It was necessary to facilitate the process of gathering information about what they knew of psychiatric services in the UK (Dein, 1997). Further, to ascertain what their experience was of working with health professionals in the community.

Figure 1: Genogram

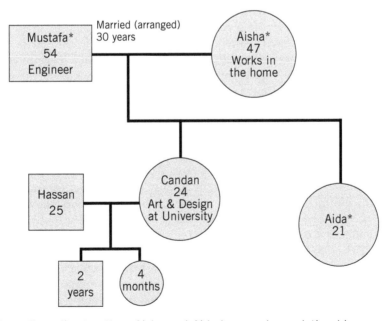

*These three live together. Aisha and Aida have a close relationship.

The assessment revealed that connected with the onset of her condition, Aida was taken to see a Muslim leader every night for three months as her family viewed her behaviour as 'uncontrollable'. The 'uncontrollable behaviour', was identified by the family as the presenting problem. It involved Aida staying out late at night and socialising with members of the opposite sex. From discussion with the family, the therapist concluded that their view was that aid from the Muslim leader to address this problem had more validity than help from health professionals. The systemic process of joining with this family from a minority ethnic group was particularly important. Utilising the technique of joining, (which involves the therapist using non-verbal communication to mirror the behaviour of the family in order to facilitate engagement) the therapist was able to accommodate to the family's style and create an environment in which family members could feel supported.

Formulating

This case shows how the work involved the co-construction of meaning with the family using systemic interventions (Goldenberg & Goldenberg, 2000). These interventions consisted of taking a stance of curiosity – where everyone's viewpoint counts (Cecchin, 1987). It was also based on the premise of circularity – feedback from the family system (Penn, 1982). Together, through 'conversation', possible alternatives to the interactional patterns they had known up to this point were created. There was a process of discovery of new ways of looking at their situation and an examination of possible solutions. As guided by post-modernist theory (Jones, 1993; Burck & Speed, 1995), the author did not attempt to exert power or control over the sessions. The author was well aware that she did not have 'the answers' when she walked into the room. Rather, she engaged the family in examining the views of others in the system, knowing that they would be in a better position to provide answers. The therapeutic goals came largely from the family's perspective of the problem. Although, the author was, undoubtedly, influenced by what the referring person had expressed and, by the questions asked, this influence found its way into the family process. The task was knowing which questions to ask in order to broaden the family's experience of one another. Further, to encourage the family to tell their story, deconstruct it and reconstruct it in a way that empowered them to change (Parry, 1993).

As noted above, transcultural therapy is not an approach in itself. Rather, it is a perspective on therapy or therapy style (D'Ardenne & Mahtani, 1989). The author found that it was possible to use a systemic theoretical framework and a transcultural perspective to the clinical work (Boyd-Franklin, 1989). In this way, the author began to formulate that it was possible that the RTA Aida suffered had been a dynamic horizontal stressor in the family's life cycle (Carter & McGoldrick, 1988: see Figure 4.1). This seemed to have catapulted the family into a pattern of relating to Aida, which made her symptomatic behaviour likely to continue to occur. Perhaps, along with genetic and organic factors, this way of responding to Aida had contributed to the presenting problem of her 'uncontrollable behaviour'.

Hypothesising

As suggested elsewhere in this chapter, therapists should seek to acquire information about a family's culture from the family itself (Wing Sue & Sue, 1999). Also, therapists should aim to expose themselves to cultural diversity both inside and outside of the therapy room (D'Ardenne & Mahtani, 1989). From information the author had previously gained from the family during the assessment phase and from an earlier inquiry into Muslim culture, the author was able to form a hypothesis on the basis of knowledge that Muslim family members often sacrifice themselves for the sake of their religion (Lau, 1994). As part of the process of working transculturally, the author began to hypothesise that Aisha was offering herself as a 'martyr' within the family by forming an enmeshed subsystem with Aida. The author tested this hypothesis out with the family [directed at the sister]:

> 'What does your Mum stand to gain from offering herself as the "martyr" when it comes to the family?'

Through Candan's response, new information was introduced into the system. Her view was,

> 'Mum thinks she would be saying she was a failure if she asked for support.'

The author began to consider that the way Aisha was positioned within the family may have been heavily steeped in cultural specifications of how a mother should cope with illness in the family. This enabled culturally sensitivity in the next utterance.

Selecting interventions

The transcultural therapist is sensitive to the need to thoughtfully select interventions which are culturally congruent for his/her client (Eleftheriadou, 1994; Wing Sue & Sue, 1999). The following intervention was designed to value the family's experience of their ethnicity, whilst still aiming to provide alternatives to the way things had been in the family up until this point. This was done by coupling a statement about how vital Islam and Muslim culture appeared to be to the family with a future-oriented question which was as follows:

> '[Directed at Candan] Given the Muslim culture you have said is important to your family, what kind of support would your Mum accept?'

Later, the author discovered that even though Mustafa was absent from the home much of the time (and did not attend sessions), other members of the family would feedback to him the occurrences of our sessions. In a Muslim family, the father is often viewed as the most influential (Lau, 1995). In line with my previous investigation into Muslim culture, it emerged that Mustafa seemed to make the final decision regarding how much the family changed in the way they related to one another. In an intervention which followed my discovery, the author summarised what members of the family had said and reflected that Mustafa seemed to make the decisions whilst being largely absent from the scene. This intervention was intended to promote enough conflict in the relationships of the family members present with Mustafa, without completely undermining his authority, and so produce change. Further, the author postulated that Mustafa's individual experiences with his family may have confirmed a belief that this is how a symptomatic woman should be responded to. It appeared that he related to Aida in much the same way as he had done his mother who suffered with schizophrenia and his depressed wife – from a distance. The author tentatively hypothesised that he was perpetuating a generational myth (Jones, 1993), as this was also how his father related to his mother (leaving her with 5 children when she became ill at 39 years old). This was identified as a vertical stressor on the system (Carter & McGoldrick, 1988: see Figure 4.1).

Managing practice dilemmas

Working transculturally, therapists are likely to face dilemmas in their practice which they might otherwise never meet. Here, the author was confronted with a situation which initially appeared as though it was a positive change in the way Aisha was relating to Aida. However, being culturally sensitive alerted me to consider the impact the proposed change might have had on the family and on the wider community.

Through liaising with my colleague, the author discovered that Aisha had approached the nurse to suggest that she look for somewhere where Aida could move to be supported in the community. According to Aisha's specifications, this would need to be a home just for females, which was outside of the Muslim community. Aisha expressed that she did not want the rest of the community to know that the family had resorted to such measures to look after one of its members. She further stated that for the time being, this would need to be kept secret from Aida and her father. Aisha reported that her fear was that if Aida knew about the change, she would inform Mustafa who would ensure that it was blocked. As alluded to above, at first this sounded like an attractive proposition. It would have meant that there was change in the system, Aida's 'uncontrollable behaviour' might become extinct and she would certainly have been physically more independent of her family. However, following further reflection on the consequences this might hold for the family, change in this direction looked less attractive. This change suggested that Aisha and the nurse had entered into a coalition which could be potentially damaging to the system (Palazzoli, Boscolo, Cecchin and Prata, 1980). Being culturally sensitive enabled me to question whether doing this Aisha was distancing herself from her family and wider culture. The questions the author planned to ask Aisha in our next session were as follows:

- How would Mustafa respond to the changes in Aisha?
- How would Aida respond to the changes in her mother (and in the relationship between her mother and father)?
- How would Candan respond to the changes in the relationship between her mother and Aida?
- How would Candan respond to the changes in the relationship between her mother and father?
- How would the Muslim community respond to the changes in the family?
- Who would gain the most/least from these changes?

In response to the above questions, Aisha and the author considered that gradually introducing change was perhaps preferable to the drastic measure of alienating herself within her family and wider community.

In summary, this section used case material based on family work from the author's own practice to illuminate the process of culturally sensitive therapy; and consider the impact of religion on the therapeutic process. It provided an example

Figure 5: Mohammed Family: Horizontal & Vertical Stressors

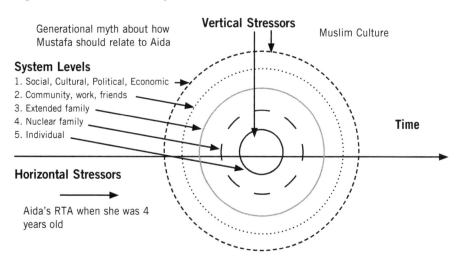

Source: Adapted from E.A. Carter and M. McGoldrick, (1988) Overview: The changing family life cycle: A framework for family therapy. In B. Carter & McGoldrick (Eds.) *The changing family life cycle: A framework for family therapy* (2nd edn). Boston: Allyn & Bacon.

of how therapists could include a consideration of cultural difference in therapy when assessing, formulating, hypothesising and selecting interventions. It also suggested how therapists might manage practice dilemmas. In presenting this case, emphasis was placed on the importance of carefully considering the family's socio-cultural context within the practice of therapy with families. In conclusion, there are some additional points to make about culturally sensitive practice. The four points listed below were adapted from Dein (1997). Culturally sensitive practice involves:

- The therapist being aware of the need to work with clients from minority ethnic groups where possible to develop his/her own confidence in working with people across different races and cultures.
- The therapist aiming to get information about racial and cultural differences directly from clients and using terms which value people from ethnic minorities and respective cultures.
- The therapist attempting to get the client's view on the problem and beliefs about treatment.
- The therapist knowing the limitations of his/her skills and or agency and using knowledge of the availability of specialist services for minority ethnic clients to direct clients to these services as appropriate.
- The therapist appropriately using supervision as a reflective space to challenge his/her assumptions.

Dr Lorraine Gordon
Counselling Psychologist

References

Abe, K., Jennifer, S. & Takeuchi, D. (1996) Cultural competence and quality of care: Issues for mental health service delivery in managed care. *Clinical-Psychology: Science-and-Practice, 3*(4), 273–295.

Beck, A. (2016). *Transcultural cognitive behaviour therapy for anxiety and depression: A practical guide.* London: Routledge.

Bhui, K.S., Aslam, R.W., Palinski, A. et al. (2015). Interventions to improve therapeutic communications between Black and minority ethnic patients and professionals in psychiatric services: Systematic review. *The British Journal of Psychiatry, 207*(2), 95–103.

Boyd-Franklin, N. (1989). *Black families in therapy.* London: Guildford.

Burbach, F. (1996). Family based interventions in psychosis – An overview of, and comparison between, family therapy and family management approaches. *Journal of Mental Health, 5,* 2, 111–134.

Burck, C. & Speed, B. (1995). *Gender, power and relationships.* London: Routledge.

Cabral, R.R. & Smith, T.B. (2011). Racial/ethnic matching of clients and therapists in mental health services: A meta-analytic review of preferences, perceptions, and outcomes. *Journal of Counseling Psychology, 58*(4), 537–554.

Carter, E.A. & McGoldrick, M. (1988). Overview: The changing family life cycle: A framework for family therapy. In B. Carter & McGoldrick (Eds.) *The changing family life cycle: A framework for family therapy* (2nd edn.) Boston: Allyn & Bacon.

Carter, R. (1995). *The influence of race and racial identity in psychotherapy: Toward a racially inclusive model.* New York: John Wiley & Sons Inc.

Cecchin, G. (1987). Hypothesizing, circularity and neutrality revisited: An invitation to curiosity. *Family Process, 26,* 405–413.

Chao, G.T. & Willaby, H.W. (2007). International employment discrimination and implicit social cognition: New directions for theory and research. *Applied Psychology, 56,* 678–688. doi:10.1111/j.1464-0597.2007.00317.x

Cochrane, R. & Bal, S.S. (1987). Migration and Schizophrenia: An examination of five hypotheses. *Social Psychiatry, 22,* 181–191.

Commander, M.J., Sashidharan, S.P., Odell, S.M., Surtees, P.G.M.J. & Commander, M.D. (1997). Access to Mental Health Care in an Inner-city Health District. I: Pathways into and within Specialist Psychiatric Services. *The British Journal of Psychiatry, 170*(4), 312–316.

Commission for Health Improvement Clinical governance review of acute and community services and investigation into mental health services. Pembrokeshire and Derwen NHS Trust March 2004.

Cross, W.E., Parkham, T.A. & Helms, J.E. (1991). The stages of black identity development: Nigrescence models. In R.L. Jones (Ed.) *Black psychology* (3rd edn, pp.319–338). Berkeley, CA: Cobb & Henry.

D'Ardenne, P. & Mahtani, A. (1989). *Transcultural counselling in action.* London: Sage.

Dein, S. (1997). ABC of mental health: Mental health in a multiethnic society. *British Medical Journal, 315,* 473–476.

Drinane, J.M., Owen, J. & Tao, K.W. (2018). Cultural concealment and therapy outcomes. *Journal of Counseling Psychology, 65*(2), 239–246.

Eleftheriadou, Z. (1994). *Gateways to counselling: Transcultural counselling.* London: Central Book Publishing.

Fernando, S. (1988). *Race and culture in psychiatry.* London: Croom Helm.

Fernando, S. (1995). (Ed.) *Mental health in a multi-ethnic society.* London: Routledge.

Fernando, S. (2010). *3rd Ed Mental Health, Race and Culture.* Palgrave: Macmillan.

Fung, K., & Lo, T. (2017) An integrative clinical approach to cultural competent psychotherapy. *Journal of Contemporary Psychotherapy, 47*(2), 65–73.

Furnham, A. & Bochner, S. (1986). *Culture shock. Psychological reactions to unfamiliar environments.* Methuen & Co. Ltd.

Goodwin, A. & Power, R. (1986). Clinical psychology services for ethnic minority groups. *Clinical Psychology Forum, 5,* 24–28.

Goodwin, B.J., Coyne, A.E. & Constantino, M.J. (2018). Extending the context-responsive psycho-therapy integration framework to cultural processes in psychotherapy. *Psychotherapy, 55*(1), 3–8.

Jones, E. (1993). *Family systems therapy: Developments in the Milan-Systemic therapies.* Chichester: John Wiley & Sons.

Kareem, J. & Littlewood, R. (Eds.) (1992). *Inter-cultural therapy, themes, interpretations and Practice.* London: Blackwell.

Lago, C. & Thompson, J. (1996). *Race, culture and counselling.* Buckingham: Open University Press.

Lau, A. (1994). Transcultural issues in family therapy. *Journal of Family Therapy, 6,* 91–112.

Lau, A. (1995). Gender, power and relationships: ethno-cultural and religious issues. In C. Burck & B. Speed (Eds.) *Gender, power and relationships.* London: Routledge.

NHS Executive Mental Health Task Force (1994). Black mental health – a dialogue for change. Department of Health: London.

Palazzoli, M.S., Boscolo, L., Cecchin, G. & Prata, G. (1980). The problem of the referring person. *Journal of Marital and Family Therapy, 6*(1), 3–9.

Penn, P. (1982). Circular questioning. *Family Process, 21,* 267–280.

Pinderhughes, E. (1990). Legacy of slavery: The experience of Black families in America, In Marsha Pravder Mirkin (Ed.) *The social and political contexts of family therapy.* Boston, MA: Allyn & Bacon, Inc.

Schen, C.R. & Greenlee, A. (2018). Race in supervision: Let's talk about it. *Psychodynamic Psychiatry, 46*(1), 1–21.

Sue, D.W. & Sue, D. (1999). (3rd edn.) *Counselling the culturally different: Theory and practice.* John New York: Wiley & Sons Inc.

Reflections of therapy

Yannick Nyah

Introduction and meanings

I understand that the word therapy can be substituted for care, treatment, and related medical interventions so I hope to begin by looking at some definitions of therapy in order to understand what may be meant by the question as well as inform my own perspective and understanding.

> 'These orientations all focused less on the unconscious and more on promoting positive, holistic change through the development of a supportive, genuine, and empathic therapeutic relationship.'

Rollo May, Carl Rogers, and Irvin Yalom
acknowledge The Influence of Otto Rank 1884–1939.

It is generally accepted that a therapeutic or medical treatment is the attempted remediation of a health problem, usually following a diagnosis. By diagnosis, I presuppose to mean identifying the nature and cause of a certain phenomenon, with variations in the use of logic, analytics and experience to determine 'cause and effect'. I also attempt to understand that in medicine in general, an indication is a valid reason to use a certain test, medication, procedure, or surgery. There can be multiple indications to use a procedure or medication. An indication can commonly be confused with the term diagnosis.

A diagnosis is a particular medical condition while an indication is a reason for use. The opposite of an indication is a contraindication, a reason to withhold a certain medical treatment because the risks of treatment clearly outweigh the benefits. Furthermore, treatment and therapy are generally used interchangeably. However, in the context of mental health and the question set before me, would it be fair to subtract that the term therapy on this occasion may refer specifically to psychotherapy?

To begin with, I have a problem, my capacity to understand all these definitions, put them together to formulate meaning for myself of what is meant by the question asked (i.e. my experiences of therapy) and thus subsequently answer to the best of my know how but I will try. Let me start with an NHS definition I find linguistically easier to read, understand, and subtract applied value from:

According to NHS Inform,

> 'Psychotherapy is a type of therapy used to treat emotional problems and mental health conditions. It involves talking to a trained therapist, either one-to-one, in a group or with your wife, husband or partner …

I ask … why not children?

> It allows you to look deeper into your problems and worries, and deal with troublesome

habits and a wide range of mental disorders, such as depression and schizophrenia. Psychotherapy usually involves talking, but sometimes other methods may be used – for example, art, music, drama and movement. Psychotherapy can help you discuss feelings you have about yourself and other people, particularly family and those close to you. In some cases, couples or families are offered joint therapy sessions together.

You will meet your therapist regularly, usually once a week, for several months, or some-times even years. Individual sessions last about 50 minutes, but group sessions are often a bit longer.'

https://www.nhsinform.scot/tests-and-treatments/counselling-and-therapies/psychotherapy

To make matters even more interesting, I have not been able to find any legally enforced regulation of counselling and psychotherapy in the UK. Joining a professional body and adhering to an ethical code is voluntary. In addition, the titles of 'Counsellor' and 'Psychotherapist' are not protected, therefore there is no legal minimum qualification needed to practice under those titles. That been said, most employers, require a minimum qualification of Level 4 diploma in counselling.

Whether statutory legislation is necessary or not, is not a subject much debated by counselling and psychotherapy in my short research. At present, there are no specific plans for a change in the law, and no universally agreed answer about how counselling and psychotherapy should be regulated in the UK.

To draw a short conclusion from all the above, it is difficult for me to say what therapy is from written definitions. I propose to define therapy now from what I think I would mean by it given my experiences.

Therapy has been my family member listening to me at odd hours of the day when I repeat the same conversations and challenges that intoxicate me time and time again. Therapy has been a collection of moments with my friends, family, colleagues and strangers too, at any given location whereby we have connected and I have shared something which I am having difficulty with and the person has listened without judging me from their own experience but simply facilitated a qualitative ear and temperament at that moment.

The above has come from formal and informal settings and relationships with a network of people, some of whom would probably not remember today.

Background

The below sums up my experience of the outcomes of all modes of therapy, it captures in a way I could not possibly write about again as my mind set will be very different. This email is what I consider the remnants of childhood trauma, written at a time when suicidal thoughts were prominent in my mind.

Dear all,

The date is 20th February 2015 and the time is 1.42am as I begin to write this. As you are aware, I have been seeing a counsellor/therapist in relation to alcoholism, depression and mental wellbeing which I started in September 2014.

The program began with a measured and gradual reduction in consumption, followed by suggestions to deal with the reasons behind my drinking to minimise relapsing coupled with ideas on coping mechanisms. The initial advice was to inform my family then discuss with them my feelings around how they can support me to avoid situations that lead me to drink.

By the end of September, I was able to wake up and not feel the need to consume alcohol in order to cope with the day. I had been sober up until two weeks ago. I have managed to detox again, starting from day one.

I am unsure of where to begin … so I will just write as it comes … I realise that there is so much unfolding at the moment and everyone makes me question my timing – over the past few months, Denise has often asked me to talk, it was not about been ready or not, but just content. Whilst my impulse and conditioning is to apologise and not speak, I am going to be very selfish. In the past, I would lie to myself and suppress it, believing that I am ok. Some of what I am about to write will be hurtful, rude, ungrateful …

Over the past 15 years, I have gathered so much debt and guilt which has caused me to not be able to sleep and so I drink heavily and happily … taking on the illusion that it does not matter. Having not finished university which I lied about elaborately to you and Lette, I have carried that shame with me – I remember that we were the dull children that should not have been brought here in the first place. A defining moment in my life was coming back to [.....] after [......] and sleeping with a woman in the living room whilst Bridgett whom was my partner at the time was in the house. I think you said it was stupid to me, you were diluting – as it was immoral. I remember feeling so ashamed that I could not even open the door when you came to see me to face you Lette. As you had been a guarantor for our flat, I have not forgotten that you were threatened with litigation as the rent had not been paid for some time. The reason you were also able to resolve this was because of some technicality.

Then came my relationship with Jan, the move to [......] which you advised against. Lette, I remember an event near [......] which I attended with David and Jan. At the time, Andrea was in [......] and worked for you, whilst we were flirting you left your seat and asked her to stay away from me – you warned me about her. We recently spoke because Andrea called you to ask you to make sure that I continued to repay the loan from her to avoid taking me to court again.

Then came the visit to [......] in 2009 and the resulting passport issue followed now by the problems you hear concerning Berth and I. Whilst these are events that live in me, I am sure there are others which I probably have not said that you may remember. I do not know of or think anyone else has caused you so much headache as I have.

Denise, I remember you calling me whilst I was at university to warn me not to destroy Terry's credit rating (your son was the word you used) as I had taken a student overdraft in his name. When the bank statement came, you opened it and asked Terry, who explained he was trying to help me out. I have also not forgotten one of our trips to [......] to visit uncle Ted. At that time, I took eggs from his fridge and put it in our bag without asking – you felt embarrassed.

As has been the case with my relationships, you also have had to endure, educate and nurse me back to a degree of wellbeing following my breakup with Jan, and me feeling sorry for myself. I recall the time when you worked 2 jobs – night and day, struggling so Terry and I will not miss out. Again, there are relentless times that I have caused you heartache – be it with Bridgett, Berth or simply just by my lack of honesty and openness with you.

Dear Stephanie, it was wrong of me to speak to you in the way I did, swear at you and ask you leave my house. My reference to children was inconsiderate and the manner in which I deliberately treated you is regretful. I was angry, spiteful and very bitter. Most importantly for me sis is the concern that you see in my eyes when you look at me, the worry that you feel which I know causes all of you the most pain as well as disappointment and shame. I feel loved by you all and know that you all love me deeply even though I put you through so much – that will never change.

I would now like to go back and talk about some of the emotions which I think I have suppressed. It's just my take on how things have unfolded for me. This is difficult to write and I think to read.

Before coming to [......], from what I have been told, we lived in [......], then [......]. Whilst in [......], I have stayed in [......], [......], [......], [......] and [......]. I have never really settled in one place.

I have very happy memories of [......] when Denise, Terry and I lived together at [......] – with one exception when I ran out of the house. My happiest memory was one Christmas when sis surprised us – sega mega drive and a football. I remember going to [......] to visit uncle Jack, when you first brought me to [......], I recall dancing then crying a lot for no apparent reason. I also remember going to [......] to register for school, I was asked my name and I said YN. I remember eating sweets. As it had been explained to me, I came here as Denise's child, so I thought that was my name too.

During that time, there were a few black African children around me, and my accent was often made fun of. I also could not read or even tell the time which at my age then, most children should have … hence why you used to crack my head a lot Denise every night in bed to learn fast. I would not say I was bullied at school, but I know I did not fit in at first. However, I was very good at sports, a lot of children warmed to me but did not have any friends until Terry came. He was the most consistent aspect of everything I know so far in every way.

After some time, other African children came, my accent changed/became more accept-able and we got to know the environment. I bonded well with Jackie. Around this time, mama came to visit and I remember not wanting to speak to her. She was very keen on learning to read so she could read the bible and often wanted me to teach her. I did not like been around her and it was Terry who sat with her patiently to teach her how to read. I understood mama did not like my relationship with Jackie and her influence on me, plus given the financial situation suggested it would be better for me to move to [......]. Also, at this time, I played a lot of sports and was particularly good at hockey. My PE teacher had written to Denise to ask her if she would be open to speaking with the county hockey club as they were interested in me doing some trials. Denise, you dictated the letter but asked me to write back and say that it would be fine – along with piano lessons, you seized every opportunity to teach with no money. During the week of trials, I was dropped home for 3 consecutive days at about 10.30pm and was so tired, you said it was too much.

A couple of days after that, you sat me down in your room and asked me how I felt about going to live in [......], I remember just crying. You and Terry also cried. You explained you did not want me to go ... I remember that like yesterday. I remember been put on the train. I cried so much, one woman sitting next to me tried her best to console me. Back then, I feared uncle Leon a lot because he was very strict and authoritative, I also had not really known sis Lette – she had always been abroad.

When I got to [......], sis Lette took me to do a test for Grammar school but I did not pass so we registered for a high school about 20 minutes walk from the house. At the time, my school had 2 or 3 black people. Most of the children lived locally, had gone to nursery and primary school together, had the same accent, 2 parent families and definitely did not like African accents. I remembered lying to everyone that I lived with my mum, brother (Troy) and sister (Kerry).

At home, sis aked me to make a timetable and put it up on the wall in the kitchen. My chores were to make sure Kerry and Troy were ready for school on time, have breakfast and clean up before I go to school. When I got back, I had to call sis to check what dinner would be, and start preparations, do my homework, make sure Troy did his, either remove the washing from the washing machine or fold those clothes outside or on the radiator/airer. Once we had eaten, to make sure that all plates were washed, dried and put away, the kitchen cleaned before watching TV and then go to bed. On Saturdays, vaccum and dust, Sundays do the ironing. This was no different to you in many ways – familiarity.

I used to hate it when school finished because I had to come home when all other chil-dren could not wait for it to end. This is when I started drinking alcohol. I would steal it from the pantry or some beer from the washroom. Uncle Leon often told me off about it saying he knew how many was there. As sis used to give me £40 a month pocket money, I would buy cider, hide it in my room and drink before I go to bed. I remember been caught one time with a lot of bottles in my room – I lied it was for a science project at school, sis believed me.

Over this period, if we were running late for school, sis Lette would walk past me calling me a slow coach. Most of the time, I would be sitting at the bottom of the stairs sorting out my school bag – I understand that she wanted me to do things faster but at the time it did not feel that way. If uncle Leon's shirts were not ironed properly, he would put them back in the basket for me to redo. I was allowed to use the normal iron but not the steam iron.

When we had visitors or went to visit anyone, it was usually aunty Kelly and uncle Rick or aunty Fiona and her husband – all mum and dad with children families – nuclear family. Over Christmas, there would be many presents for children and a couple for me. If there were telephone calls, people would ask about them. During this time, I would spend any of my spare time in my room.

By the time, I left to go to University, I had made friends and could not wait to be free. On the first day, everyone's mum and dad turned up to drop them off. During half term, it was the same. At University, I met girls and would go out most nights clubbing and miss lectures. As girls seemed to be attracted to me, a lot of guys would hang around me. I passed the first year to go unto the second year. In my second year, I met a girl called Dela who was local, I thought I fell in love. I then started going to expensive bars and clubs because that was what she and the people around me liked – I spent most of my student loan buying her gifts, I wanted her to like me so much. Because everyone thought she was pretty, it made me feel like I fitted in somewhere. We smoked weed and tried cocaine. She then broke up with me and I was so miserable, I came to back to [......] to visit Denise.

Going back to university, I was angry with women and felt rejected deciding to teach them all a lesson and ended up getting gonorrhoea. Sis Lette arranged for me to attend a clinic for treatment and some counselling. Once again feeling very ashamed of myself knowing that Sis Lette would bring home condoms and leaflets and tell me off, I turned to drinking to cover up what an insecure idiot and a mess I was. After some time, Bridgett comes into the picture and in hindsight, my womanising and drinking became habitual for coping but was not uncontrollable.

When I meet Jan, we shared so much lust that I finally believed again that someone could like me but the truth is she liked the person I showed her and wanted to be. Her parents bought a house in [......] which they put under our names until she discovered I had slept with Andrea, slowly but surely that comes to an end. We start a business which she cannot be bothered to come to work for and is always me there and when we get a contract, things change. Whilst in Ireland, I learn that some people have never seen a black person other than on tv and they want to touch me like am on exhibition and get shouted at – 'you, black bastard walking on the street'.

When I move back to [.......], it takes a while, but I stop drinking, focus and work as hard as I can. I outperform the entire stockbroking firm consistently enough for them to pay for my exams. The support that Sis Denise and Terry give at this time makes me feel safe. As sis starts to date her ex, he offers Terry and I some shirts – Terry accepts but I don't. My reason is because Jan call had me a scavenger when we broke-up, when she is speaking with sis Denise as she wants to find out what happened, she told you how it was her family who paid for everything (yes I know what Berth feels like). I set my mind that I will never take anything from anyone in order to stop that feeling.

Sis Denise felt I was been disrespectful to her and her partner and calls me on the morning of my 3rd and final stockbroking exam which allows me to become FSA registered broker to move out of her house. I call Stephanie who allows me to move in with her. Sis Lette then calls me to say that I should have been considerate.

This brings me to Carly, who I started dating at the time and comes from a wealthy family – she owned her own house, car etc and wanted me to move in with her – I refused because I had learnt a lesson and made myself a promise. In addition to that, I begin to think culture even within Africans makes a difference.

I pass the exam, I qualify and become a senior broker and move out of Stephanie's. At this stage, it has been decided that we all go to [......] as a family for once and Henvy is opening. I refuse given my situation at work, only just having been promoted and because my passport had not been stamped.

Sis Lette called me to advice that it is very important and explained how disappointed she would be if I do not go. I contact immigration who advised that so long as I have the letter stating indefinitely leave then I would be allowed back into the country.

As I could not come back, it was made clear at the time that this was once again my irresponsibility and Sis Lette expressed concerns as to whether I had sold the previous passport and once again not to put her into difficulty particularly from a legal position. Sis Denise called me to say it was my own stupidity and I should resolve the issues myself as she was tired of picking up my rubbish. I recall mum begging and crying on the phone without really knowing what I had put everyone through to help. Stephanie called to find out what could be done.

Whilst in [......], uncle Leon helped me to sort out some work which kept me busy at the hospital and I also assisted with admin in Henvy. During the day, everyone usually went to school and so it would be dad, mum, and me. The conversation between dad and I were advisory or explanatory in regard to tradition and customs and with mum it was about cooking – an attempt to understand her son, becoming so protective as I did not know the environment. This was useful for our bonding. It also highlighted to me that they do not know me any more than I know them – so many links and experiences missing. Mum often said she could not understand what I was saying and even in my time there referred to some of my habits as 'white man culture'.

In [......] I was an exhibition and now in [......] I am also an exhibition – the bush fellow that you know, knew but I am a stranger to them. I don't fit in there and not here either. My own mother cannot understand my literal words. 90% of my conversation with my father revolves around me providing him with money. My relationship with our parents has been so one way that sometimes I wonder why. We have practical conversations.

I have been a very needy and difficult child to care for and based solely on the snapshot above, that seems euphemistic. I recognise and envy stability and emotional freedom/ licence that a mother (parents) can provide for their children. If you cannot communicate freely with your own mother, who can you really do that with even she is alive, and it is not that you have a problem with one another?

We come from a very hierarchical culture/family discriminating almost naturally with age and gender/money/status. Sis Lette and I spoke about Jeff's christening and making sure enough time is provided to ensure that someone like aunty Kate is consulted and available. My understanding of that is, she has been there for you which allowed you to be there for us. I still see sis Denise today calling you over Christmas and New Year to thank you and Stephanie too – falling in line and I sincerely ask myself when does gratitude become indebtedness and what the difference between that and slavery is?

During family gatherings and speeches, if referring to me, quite a few of you make a claim to be my mother, a question I have actually given thought to. The truth as I know and accept, is that my mother is mum. Over the last 3 years, I hear from different people about what this person has given/done for me. That shackles me, I would rather not have and be forced to find alternatives – this is better for my mental wellbeing.

Until today, I have very little memories of childhood in [......] particularly time with mum and dad. I have tried to be open as much as I could and even now ... I fear the repercussions. This is what I meant by being emotionally unsafe sis Denise. I simply never feel this way with Terry.

My money situation can be managed, and I am working at that too, I am not working but I trade sufficiently to add to housing benefit to pay the rent at least. I do not like to come around – this is to do with guilt and shame. I feel safer being alone because I have to drink every time I am around family. The idea of Jeff growing up without access to me or Berth is my priority. Hopefully the counselling will allow me to become a better person and as I probably require a personality transplant, this will take some time. I believe that gifts come at a premium and nothing is for free. I think only parents owe you anything and nobody else.

My sincere interest at the moment is electromagnetism and genetics which I have begun to teach myself step by step.

I will always love you.

My relationship and experience with psychotherapists and therapy

Whilst 'dual relationships' are typically frowned upon publicly by the mental health community and are even more challenging to manage, and would struggle to meet moral and ethical standards, my own experience with professional therapists was often distant and detached, automatic and lacked trust perhaps on both sides. Those I considered close friends would take the place of what the British Association for Counselling and Psychotherapy (BACP) may want to call a trained practitioner and by that application, I would probably not be alive today as someone whom has attempted suicide.

Through the course of my life, friends have provided key effective interventions. Coming from West Africa whereby therapy is unheard of, culturally relevant advice or church is preferred. It often 'takes a village' and the idea behind this is that, society provides my therapy. So, I would actually prefer to examine as feedback, how the professional therapeutic environment can better take into account the intersectional links between all options available to me to utilise as I the patient see fit for my wellbeing objectives and adopt or recognise the full picture.

Would it be possible to make this both practical and ethical for a friend or relative to facilitate this type of care in line with academically trained therapists? Or should the therapists be trained to access what a friend does and what would that look like? It seems, I would like to make a case for better informative relations in all circumstances.

> *'It is much easier to talk to a stranger than to sit down and talk about certain personal issues with someone who knows you. Part of your self-respect is to promote a healthy picture of yourself to friends, not to show all the eyesores that only you can see on the inside'.*

Student quoted in Leach 2015

If I assume therapy to be the treatment of physical, mental, social disorders or disease, more specifically under the BACP umbrella term:

> *'Counselling and psychotherapy are umbrella terms that cover a range of talking therapies. They are delivered by trained practitioners who work with people over a short or long term to help them bring about effective change or enhance their wellbeing'.*
> British Association for Counselling and Psychotherapy (BACP)

As well as taking into account Sociologist Graham Allen's study in 2008, suggesting that there are at least three key features in maintaining a friendly relationship:

> *'shared interests, equality and reciprocity and that we form friendships with other people because we like them. However, those friendships are only likely to persist if both parties share enough of a common outlook, are roughly equal in terms of their social and economic status and are able to give and take in providing mutual support. People may be changed by their friendships, but this is not usually the main reason for engaging in them'.*

Graham Allen's 2008 study

If friendships are about having fun and for some people part of preserving a friendship may consist of taking their problems to a professional instead, what if you don't have friends or know your problems or that you have a problem particularly the case when you are a child mindful of developmental age and severity of issues.

In contrast to my friendships, my relationship with trained therapists has not been based on shared experiences, interests and values, trusts as such, intimacy, or deeper understanding, other than a potential 'successful' outcome of the therapy for the therapists feel good factor. The relationship has not been based on equality of status or reciprocity which I personally believe are important for shared understanding to awaken.

My therapeutic relationships require clearly stated time limits and boundaries to the relationship, whereas in friendships and amongst my family members and strangers alike, the boundaries are less clear and are often up for negotiation – this was the problem I encountered one night and it pushed me to relapse whereby a friend could not absorb any more due to their own mental health challenges. What is said in the consulting room is classed as private and confidential and so may encourage discussion of topics that it would be too embarrassing to mention to friends but without a certain comfort zone, I am unable to open up regardless of the person or people, training or setting.

The structured approach used by the therapists I encountered, adopted as a consequence of training based on psychological theories, and supervised practice did not facilitate comfort and a setting poised to evoke that type of conversation but much like that of an interview.

There is a very strange counter argument I make to myself which is, I was not ready maybe for a therapeutic relationship in the clinical sense but yet needed therapy. Whilst my friends and I through the course of my experiences have inter-acted with each other in an intuitive manner, it is highly unlikely that I or they apply a structured and theory-based approach to our relationship particularly when a true friend indeed or is in need.

As the Founding Director of an organisation that combines both informal and planning for formal bespoke therapy arrangements, therapy is what special needs parents provide for one another at various coffee mornings I have been a part of. When another parent or friend is experiencing mental distress, we tend to rely on our own experiences and understanding to provide help and support, some of which may work better than others. For me, this has more to do with lack of adequate, affordable and culturally conscious and sensitive trained therapists. The idea of therapy absent of the whole of society approach given the interconnec-tivity of challenges external to the treatment room concerns me. Therapy alone is unable to provide the holistic and pragmatic care or mitigate external factors and natures desire from my own experiences.

Although friends and family may not be officially 'qualified' to support someone in distress, there is no doubt that their help can be greatly valued as I have witnessed first-hand and delivered to others too. Just being listened to can be very supportive, as can be the provision of companionship and distractions from worry:

> *'My friends who were there to talk, to make me cups of tea, to share their experiences or just take my mind off things with a silly movie and lots of cake!'*
>
> Service user quoted in Leach 2015

Lone illness

I have been told that lone illness is considered to be the oldest mental health condition. Is this the case and if so, can a trained professional do anything about my lone illness other than to advise me on things I already know I should be doing or capable of learning? If lack of motivation is my underlying challenge, how would this work long term? Do I just top up on my short term counselling/therapy and over time and by default that becomes the psychotherapy? How is success measured to show that trained versus untrained is more effective? Is the profession a con given most of the world does not utilise a trained therapist and most people of the world would not know what that is! Are they suffering from mental health challenges or spiritual and moral lacking?

Family have helped me out in other ways too, such as providing practical support (finance, driving, babysitting, respite) and advice, and helping me to access other forms of support when the need arose but often this was problematic as they would not entirely feel comfortable to do so or I was not ready or both or more reasons than I can write. My friends have done more than give me hugs and suggest fun things to do as well as providing a sympathetic ear.

Research on informal support indicates the value of being alongside the person in distress, taking their situation seriously, but without making it seem too catastrophic, and reminding the person of the small but positive steps they can take towards greater wellbeing through doing everyday activities such as going for a walk or watching a light-hearted film (Borg & Davidson, 2008).

Trained therapists and professionals should be better equipped and supported to perform their role than friends in theory. These may include having a robust quantitative and qualitative feedback process, a statistical index similar to an equities exchange per client or me measuring factors which specifically impact me, and chart so we can measure or at least begin somewhere! Opening up about difficult emotional issues for a child with my background whereby childhood trauma, civil war, migration, poverty, feelings of abandonment, legacy of 1961, still impacts. It is difficult to filter through cultural and social factors as well as specific to my family challenges such as respect and fear of one's elders mindful of p's and q's, having capacity to be open and transparent and comfortable doing so is quite a task.

It has taken over 12 years of devout endeavour, multiple relapses to be able to identify new ways of thinking about problems and challenging self-defeating beliefs and behaviours.

Taking everything into account it would seem that you don't have to be your friend's 'therapist' in order to help them and, in fact, you can be more helpful by being a good friend to them in a number of ways that a therapist cannot.

Race

The question of race in therapy is a subject I prefer not to discuss in detail at the time of writing. What I would briefly like to ask is the mind set of those, their parents and grand-parents, family and friends that produced these important and invaluable stepping-stones and think about the degree to which an entire research program will mitigate these factors. Can these studies undertaken at the time they were undertaken, given the race, equality, political, social and spiritual challenges at the time bequeath averages that apply to me? Could this be a tragic contradiction of psychology in failing to appreciate the complexities of the mind, body and spirit?

I conclude with the following; it is because of one counselling psychologist I am able to write this otherwise I would not be able to. I find it a balanced therapeutic style in a natural setting in line with me and appropriate at the time of delivery but has been facilitated by more than their clinical 'know how' from my point of view and something to do say about the person behind the friend, family or therapists, psychotherapists or care giver at the hour needed. It matches almost all factors and mind sets I would personally require, to facilitate a type of behavioural and mental development which is different but equally necessary for my holistic wellbeing.

My experiences and probably those I have worked with or come across is very limited to draw any meaningful quantitative and logically applied general outcome values from. What I hope it can do, is give an insight which is often absent or perhaps to those around the table pertaining to care from real short, medium and long effects and their outcomes unedited with a view it may inform and contribute.

Graciously thank and enjoy therapy and psychotherapy because, I believe, the subject and its truly well-meaning followers is highly vocational and needed absent of religion. Without it, we have people in villages in Pinyin killing each other pertaining to some held hatred of conflicts gone before. If we both put down the weapons, what happens!

Psychotherapy has provided a resource in the sum of what it endeavours to do for me to read and follow and adjust like any other person. I find that it is because of this, that, different and other types of development within myself have been able to unfold.

Yannick Nyah
Founding Director of BlackMajor

Can I please have White skin too?

Faisal Mahmood

Birthday wish
Dear Mummy and Daddy,
Can I please have white skin like my friends at school?

(5 year old girl's birthday wish)

I often hear comments like; 'let's celebrate diversity' or 'I am here to learn from you (about your culture)'. I think these are perfectly reasonable statements, if you choose to work at a somewhat superficial level with your clients, or, you are restricted by your working context, or, perhaps not trained or supported enough to work any differently. It is worrying that most counselling/psychotherapy training courses still have a rather tokenistic approach towards working with ethnic minorities. It is useful to invite a specialist facilitator to run a weekend workshop but often this isn't sufficient nor effective unless working with difference is embedded throughout the training and clinical practice.

Now what is wrong with those two statements? Let's celebrate diversity! What is there to celebrate about our histories of oppression, exploitation, murderous rage, terrorism, slavery, and concentration camps? I am an Asian Muslim Gestalt Psychotherapist. I have experienced racism in many forms; usually very subtle and almost always as a surprise. I want to briefly share my personal experience to support an understanding of why I can find it a bit offensive when I hear the words 'let's celebrate diversity'.

After each Islamist terrorist attack, I struggle to sleep for days. I feel deeply embarrassed about my existence. I feel like a burden to others around me. I feel tiny when I walk on the streets of London or Birmingham or sit in a park with my children or eat fish and chips with friends in a pub. I become acutely conscious of my existence as a Muslim man wondering what impact I have on others around me. I feel apologetic when other passengers on trains look at me and wonder about my laptop bag or rucksack. To make it easier for other passengers, I deliberately open my bag fully and get out a pen or something random and then I hear a sigh of relief. I notice how many around me are carefully watching the contents of my bag. During those days, certain moments are even harder. In those moments, I kind of lose a sense of space, time and distance – I find myself asking unbearable questions: What is Islam to me? Who am I as a Muslim? And then the most painful question – Do I believe that Islam is a peaceful religion? Is the Quran really an unedited book of God? Does Allah only care about Muslims? It is in these doubts I find some peace.

I do not want my therapist to celebrate my differences. I want her to sit with my shame and anger. I want her beside me when I grapple my doubts. I think the world will have to wait years if not centuries before it can claim to celebrate diversity.

Now let's explore the second statement: 'I am here to learn from you about your culture'. This is so commonly used in our field. I have heard it many times from my therapists over the years. Each time, it felt as if it was my responsibility to teach my therapist about 'our' differences. As if I represent and embody the phenomenon of being 'different'. There are two different people in the therapy room. Being different belongs to both – client and therapist. Therapists need to learn to expand their capacity to stay with being different, stay with not getting their clients' cultural references, stay with their own curiosities and making their differences the focal point of therapeutic investigation. I am not suggesting that it is not helpful to learn about different cultural practices or norms. It is perfectly reasonable and required of therapists to expand their knowledge of different cultures for their own learning. However, I am asking therapist to be aware of the times when they generalise limited knowledge or stereotype their clients.

Cultural competency training events are absolutely useful practice to some extent. What does it even mean to be culturally competent? That I gain knowledge about other cultures – such as their religious events i.e. Vaisakhi, Holi, Eid, Rosh Hashanah etc. I think such information can be very useful, just as useful as to learn about recent cricket events if you are working with a client who plays cricket professionally. However, imagine a cultural competency event where a trainer wants to support your understanding about Muslim clients. Any discussion about Islamic beliefs or rituals can only support a position of judgement and could impact your phenomenological attitude. Some Muslim women choose to wear hijab some choose not to. Wearing the hijab has different reasons attached to it – at one extreme you have some women who are forced to wear a hijab because of family pressures and at the other end some women who make the decision for themselves. Not all Muslim women who wear hijab pray five times a day whereas there are many women who don't wear hijab but consistently pray five times a day. So who is really a true practicing Muslim? And who decides? Deciding who is a practicing Muslim is just a judgement and even Muslims have different opinions of what constitutes this. We can't discard the fact that culture and religion are deeply intertwined too. A Muslim from Saudi Arabia and a Muslim from India may have different beliefs. There are many sects in Islam and each sect holds strong negative beliefs about each other.

What do you do if your client asks you a question? Imagine you are a White therapist and your client is Black. How would you respond to your client if they ask the following question:

How do you feel about working with me?

Notice – what is your first reaction? How do you feel? Notice your body – what do you experience in your body? How are you breathing?

How would you respond to your client? Would you say something like ....

'silence .... (followed by) how do you feel about it?'

'I notice you asked me a question, but we are here for you, not for me'

'I really like working with clients who are different, I really celebrate diversity'

'I have worked with many black clients and every client is unique'

'I treat all my clients equally (so it doesn't affect me that you are black)'

None of the above responses truly fits a relational approach. Where many therapists claim that they consider therapeutic relationship as the core of their work, they often fail to demonstrate this in their clinical practice. If one claims to work in a relational manner, then they must submit to relational demands. One must not duck difficult questions. In such situations, a therapist's presence is required instead of absence. Being available to yourself, to your client and to the relationship (Joyce & Sills, 2014) is a challenging task and needs a real commitment to learn to stay with. Suspending any desire to move, change, avoid or heal, requires courageous stillness or as Gestaltists say, 'creative indifference'!

Here are some possible suggestions:

- I have mixed responses… I feel excited and interested in working with you and at the same time I notice how I am searching in my head how to best respond to you.
- I am happy to respond to you. However, I believe this question is for both of us to explore together. How do we sit with our racial differences?
- I feel careful… I am wondering about the statement behind your question.
- I suddenly notice how my heart beat increased. I am not entirely sure how to respond to your question. I notice my hesitation in saying that I am looking forward to working with you – as if it doesn't really address the question behind your question.

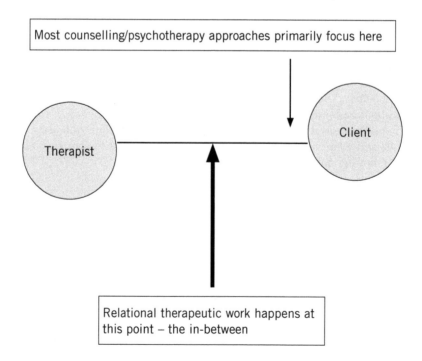

It's not surprising that many therapists move away from a truly relational place because their primary focus is their client. Many therapeutic approaches rely on an empathic attitude. This can be problematic because empathy relies on imagining, as if, what is going on for clients. The notion of empathy is primarily based on an individualistic client view (or dualistic world view). It is not surprising therefore, that it has been given a central position in counselling/psychotherapy approaches that are mainly based on western cultural norms and are inherently individualistic.

For a true relational approach (dialogical approach) the focus is not just the client but the therapist and the space in-between the two. It requires not ducking any personal challenging questions. It involves making your own phenomeno-logical experiences available to yourself and to your clients, in the service of your clients. Therapy is simply an expression of vulnerability on the part of the thera-pist. The key question is: 'can I allow myself to feel, experience, and name my own shame, anger, distance, love, judgments, boredom, and rage in the therapy room?'

How do I feel sitting with someone who is different? What meaning do I make of my whiteness in the presence of a Black client? The notion of otherness has been discussed a lot recently in the counselling/psychotherapy literature. I don't get it! Who and what is other? The one who is different in certain ways – race, religion, gender, sexuality etc? Who initiates this otherness? One in the position of privilege, perhaps a therapist? (Bartoli et al., 2015; Dottolo & Kaschak, 2015). Ryde (2009, p.15) suggests some really pertinent questions:

– Who I am as a white person?
– What is the nature of my privilege as a white person?
– How does being white affect my ability to relate to people who are not white?
– What is the nature of race?
– Who am I in a racialised environment?

So, am I saying that therapists almost always initiate otherness? No, of course I am not saying this. Often a person in a privileged position (White, British, Man, Middleclass) is seen as making the other 'the other'. Really! Many people who follow such a theory collude with oppressing field conditions that only a White British Middleclass Heterosexual Man could have such a power of making someone 'the other'. Now if 'the other' means 'different' – then that is factually correct. There is a Black person and there is a White person. They are different based on their skin colour. This is a physical fact. So what is the issue here? Are we using a noun for what really should be considered a verb? I am wondering whether the word 'othering' fits better here i.e. the dynamic interplay between two people that is constantly changing: a co-created othering.

Co-created othering is a notion that involves both parties (White-Black, Ther-apist-Client) to engage in the process of adjusting to see other and responding to their own individual and collective field conditions. It is in this precise moment, where I am sitting opposite to a White person with my history of my life and generational traumas, I regulate my contact with the other person. This contact, between me and the other person, in this very precise moment is influenced by everything that has ever happened to both of us and whatever is going in the world. Merleau-Ponty (1962) describes it well 'the lived present holds a past and a future within its thickness'.

I suggest the following steps to working relationally with ethnic minorities. This is in no way a prescriptive model nor should it be considered as a treatment manual.

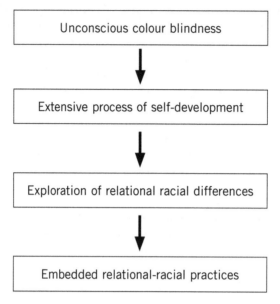

Unconscious colour blindness

This is the position where one says I don't see your colour. I am not a racist. I have many Asian and Black friends. There are other differences too.

Extensive self-development: This involves real commitment to a personal journey of enhanced self-awareness. This is where one begins to deal with their own race, skin colour, culture, and notice similarities and differences with others. I believe personal therapy is paramount for this work.

Exploration of relational-racial differences

This involves naming differences in the therapy room proactively. Be aware when you say that there are no race issues in the therapy room with this client. Or when you perceive your client as similar to you, born and brought up in the UK. Race and culture seeps into any thick walls of national geography or shores of oceans. It also includes national and international politics, current world affairs and generational traumas.

Embedded relational-racial practices

This is the position where a therapist would feel settled in their own skin (literally and metaphorically) in relation to racial differences. They freely engage in the exploration of permanently dynamic aspects of the client-therapist relational space in relation to being white or black. As a therapist, one needs to let go of any desire to resolve racial tensions or suppress one's own whiteness. One must avoid any attempt to dilute the directness of client-therapist encounter by philosophical debates such as 'other differences', 'generic power or oppression issues' or 'intersectionality'.

I wonder if there are some raised eyebrows reading my cautionary comments regarding intersectionality. It is one of the hot topics of our times. In principle, I totally agree with the notion of intersectionality. However, it feeds into the notion of 'it's very complex' and therefore creates an avoidance of direct meeting.

For decades, we have seen very forceful movements in the West that inspired almost all our different counselling/psychotherapy approaches. Most of them share a common dualistic human-world perspective, that is, a person and their world are two separate entities. It suits us in separating us from others. It also supports this centuries' old illusive notion of 'I' or 'I am'. Gestalt field theory suggests a different perspective. Wollants (2012) says that a person and his/her world are inseparable – in essence one dynamic unit. We proactively impact our world and are constantly impacted by our world.

The model overleaf explores therapist-client co-created relational dynamic in the therapy room. Therapists and clients, both part of their own individual fields, co-create their therapeutic contact. Both parties influence each other and are influenced by each other. Blank screen is just a convenient and illusive myth. The ideas of blank screen, projections and transferences in a 'vacuum' are unrealistic, non-relational concepts.

Many therapists are familiar with the notion of 'bracketing off'. This is done in the service of phenomenological enquiry, so that our personal biases and judgements don't interfere with our 'listening' of our clients. Husserl (Spinelli, 2005) introduced the Greek notion of 'Epoche' as a phenomenological method. 'Epoche' or 'bracketing off' is a widely used concept in the counselling and psychotherapy field. The English translation of Epoche is 'suspension of judgement' (Merriam-Webster, 2020).

Many therapists translated this notion of bracketing off to put aside their own beliefs as well as experiences in order to be fully present to their clients. In essence, this notion of bracketing off makes sense. However, using this concept with naivety can be counterproductive. We are not required to suspend our experiences in the therapy room. We are not 'studying' the client as an object. However, we make ourselves available to the relational encounter with our clients and it requires all our experiences including judgements, biases, and preconceptions. The difference is that we hold our judgements very lightly in the service of our relational encounter with our clients. For me to be fully present and available to my clients, I need to metaphorically put aside any preconceived and premature judgements I have about them. For example, not all Asian women experience forced or arranged marriages. Your knowledge that Asian parents can be quite controlling, interfering, or family orientated could impact your work with an Asian person who did not experience such things. Actually, the principle of Epoche requires you to suspend any knowledge you gained through attending cultural competency training because the very idea that how certain cultures behave or interact leads to preconceived judgement. For example, suggesting that Asian people have a collective pronoun such as 'we' based on their closed family ties is simply a very dangerous assumption. There are thousands of Asian people in this country who do not have close links with their families or so-called communities. I think such cultural competency training events should be undertaken with some caution. In essence, they are mainly based on generalised 'interesting' information. However,

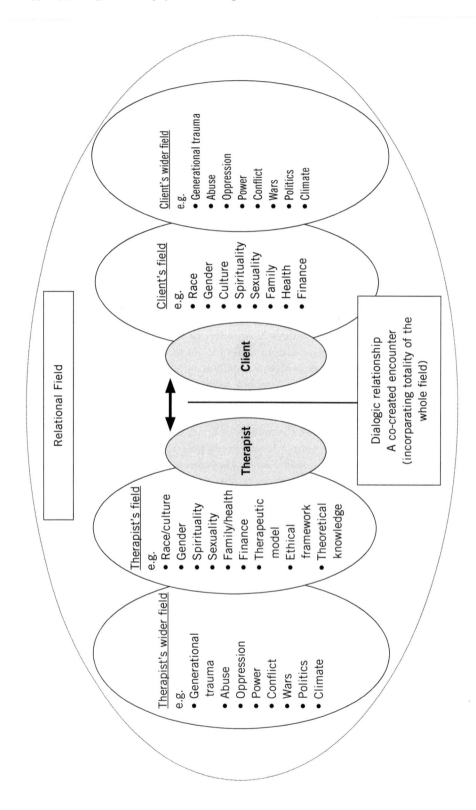

it is perfectly useful for therapists to gain knowledge about other cultures as students of social and geo-political phenomena, but these are not suggestions for their therapeutic work. When it comes to becoming more competent in working with ethnic minority clients then the focus has be on us.

Jacobs (2014) explores the issue of integration, insiders and outsiders and she says:

'I often see "African-American" and "white" juxtaposed as though they parallel terms. But the correct juxtaposition should be, "European-American". European immigrants generally drop the hyphen within a few generations because it is easier for them to be incorporated into American consciousness as "Americans". Blacks live doubly. They are quintessentially American, having been here – involuntarily, of course – from the start. And yet they are never fully "American", they remain outsiders.' (p.298)

I have lived in the UK for about 25 years now and most of my professional life spent in the counselling/psychotherapy field. This is a disproportionately white majority field. My background is in Gestalt therapy and I have not yet met with another Asian Muslim Gestalt therapist in this country. This unique position affects me in two ways. One, I stand out. This has helped me in my professional career over the years. The other is finding myself pathologically alone. Every now and then my differences become very figural to me. I feel awkward. I shut up and shut down. I suddenly feel a strong desire to join in and to be a 'normal', and perhaps to become white. I never lived in my life as a part of majority. I don't know, I mean I have no felt sense, no embodied experience of how it feels to be a part of an ethnic majority group. My parents migrated from Pakistan to Saudi Arabia. I was born in Saudi Arabia. I was a minority there. I lived a few years in Lahore, Pakistan. I was again a foreigner. I remember once being shouted at on the Ealing Broadway 'go back to your country'. Where is my country? I explored for years in my therapy my sense of groundlessness and homelessness. I guess people like me, immigrants or foreigners are fundamentally different. As if we just float on the surface. I cannot firmly rest my feet on the ground – it is as if I cannot have such a privilege. I refuse to accept any support from my environment – as if it's not mine. There is a fear that it will be taken away or I will be moved if I get too comfortable. I carry generational trauma of migration in my bones and my blood. My father, when he was 10 years old, had to migrate from India to Pakistan and lost almost all his family in that process. Over one million people were killed in the legacy of the British Raj and in the hope of inhabiting a piece of land that they could claim as theirs.

In the therapy room, when two colonized histories meet, it is important that therapists allow the impact of two contrasting pasts – oppressor and oppressed. White shame or guilt, and for that matter, empathy and desire to heal, serve as a deflection from any meaningful encounter. White shame is a process where a White person attempts to lose their own power. It is like trying to kill yourself after murdering others. I just noticed my choice of words. Unsurprisingly, I became very conscious of rage and murder whilst thinking about our colonised history. In my view, it is the therapist's task to own their power and grounded position as well as being open to witnessing and being impacted by their client.

Let me tell you about a personal experience. I received a phone voice message. It was from a client who wanted psychotherapy for her relationship issues. I called her back and we agreed to meet up for an initial mutual assessment session. The client arrived on time and I was surprised to see a Black woman. I was expecting a White client. My expectation was based on my own biases and preconceived views. She had mentioned her employment on the phone. She was in a senior high-ranking position in a local authority. Did I exhibit prejudice? Was I deeply influenced by certain pre-conceived perceptions about Black people in senior positions? Or was I a realist, basing my judgement on the fact that very few Black women are in such senior positions in this country?

She said her mother was a medically trained surgeon in an African country. Her parents came to the UK in the 1960s and her mother had to work hard to pass required medical school tests in order to work in this country. Her mother eventually left the NHS after years of harassment, discrimination and racist attitudes and started working in a local restaurant. My client said she grew up hating the colour of her skin.

In one session, she shared a very private thought with me that I still carry with me to this day and that I would like to share with you. She told me that she only had white partners and she never had dated a Black person. She hoped to have a child with a White partner and then hoped her child will also marry a White person. She said perhaps after many generations there will be no Black-ness left in her generation. She had seriously considered cosmetic procedures to change her skin colour and as she put it was 'inspired by Michael Jackson'. Did I collude with her desire when I imagined her as a White person?

I felt deeply sad and cried in the session. She shared a long list of negative experiences as a Black child living in Manchester in the 1960s and 1970s. Once, she had to crawl from her local park to her home (over 30 minutes' journey) because some older children bullied her and her younger sister while playing in the park. She never told her parents about that incident. Actually, she had never told anyone until our therapy session.

Khan (2018) reporting the findings of a WHO study for *The Guardian* noted that 40 per cent Chinese women, 61 per cent Indian women, 77 per cent Nigerian women regularly use skin-lightening creams. In 2017, the global skin-lightening industry was worth $4.8bn (£3.4bn) and in 2016, the BBC reported AC Nielsen's findings that India's whitening-cream market was worth $432m (£327m). White as beautiful, more desirable and more marketable is linked with our colonised past.

Remember

- The difference does not lie with your clients. The difference belongs to both you and your client. It is a relational phenomenon, not an individual construct. Therefore, for any meaningful therapeutic work to take place, it needs to be explored relationally.
- Empathy is essential but not sufficient. It is not just about imagining what is it like for my client or entering their world. True relational work requires empathy as well as being available to yourself, entering in your own world, your embodied responses (not just towards your client but to yourself) and finally being available to the relationship – the in-between space (a dialogic relationship). Therefore, both 'inclusion' and 'presence' are needed (Yontef, 1993).

- I am not a fixed entity nor is my client – we are constantly changing, emerging and creatively adjusting to the demands of our field conditions. Verb vs Noun! Self vs Selfing!
- Work begins with us, years of personal journey of constantly grappling with our own way of being in this world full of differences. Remember you can only take your client as far as you have travelled, or, in other words 'therapists should walk the talk' (Bennett-Levy, 2019).
- I will learn from my client – not to be used as an excuse to avoid working on yourself.
- Celebrating differences could be an avoidance of accepting the horror of racial oppression. Eating humus, samosa and curry doesn't make one more accepting of ethnic minorities.
- The question, why a Black trainee counsellor/psychotherapist does not speak much in the White majority group, doesn't belong to the Black trainee only.
- Work on your own tolerance to stay with your own fragility, shame, guilt, anger, pain, sadness, and most importantly your own power. Power shaming is simply a useful tactic to avoid relational encounter. Letting go of your privileged and powerful position in the therapy room, is not only counter-productive but also inherently oppressing.
- Avoid moving towards resolving any racial tension – stay with it. That is all that matters.
- Racism is not a myth even in this 21st century.
- If you feel your white race is 'used' against you to silence you, then acknowledge your client's desire to silence you as a function of relational response induced by history of trauma. Notice how really important it could be for your client to be in this position of speaking and silencing you.
- Embrace your own potential or actual position as a representative of an oppressing group (such as being White, Middleclass, Male). Avoid shifting to 'other' differences prematurely. It is convenient for you, if you are a White female, to move from race to gender inequalities or vice versa such as for a Black male therapist to move from gender to race inequalities. Stay still in that position of a representative of an oppressing group.
- Accept your potential to be an oppressor and to be oppressed.
- Being racially different is one of most impactful life experiences, not considering it significant enough to explore in the therapy room is simply poor therapeutic practice.
- When exploring racial differences, do not just pose questions to your clients. Questions are simply a way to avoid relational encounter.
- If you think race is used only as a political point scoring – remember that 5 years old girl's birthday wish.

Faisal Mahmood
Psychotherapist
Senior Lecturer in Counselling and Psychotherapy
Newman University
Birmingham

References

Bartoli, E., Bentley-Edwards, K.L., García, A.M., Michael, A. & Ervin, A. (2015). What do White counselors and psychotherapists need to know about race? White racial socialization in counseling and psychotherapy training programs. *Women & Therapy, 38,* 3–4, 246–262. doi:10.1080/02703149.2015.1059206

Bennett-Levy, J. (2019). Why therapists should walk the talk: The theoretical and empirical case for personal practice in therapist training and professional development. *Journal of Behavior Therapy and Experimental Psychiatry, 62*(2019), 133–145.

Dottolo, A.L. & Kaschak, E. (2015). Whiteness and White Privilege. *Women & Therapy, 38,* 3–4, 179–184. doi:10.1080/02703149.2015.1059178

Epoche. (n.d.) In Merriam-Webster's online dictionary: Retrieved 20 January 2020 from https://www.merriam-webster.com/dictionary/epoche

Jacobs, L.M. (2014). Learning to love white shame and guilt: skills for working as a white therapist in a racially divided country. *International Journal of Psychoanalytic Self Psychology, 9,* 297–312. doi:10.1080/15551024.2014.948365

Merleau-Ponty M. (1962). *Phenomenology of perception* (trans: Smith, C.). London: Routledge & Kegan Paul.

Spinelli, E. (2005). *The interpreted world: An introduction to phenomenological psychology.* (2nd edn). London: Sage Publications.

Wollants, G. (2012). *Gestalt therapy: Therapy of the situation.* London: Sage Publication Ltd.

Yontef, G.M. (1993). *Awareness, dialogue and process.* Goulsboro: The Gestalt Journal Press, Inc.